PRAISE FOR *TO DIE IN MEXICO*

"From its first shocking paragraph, this book takes the reader inside Mexico's drug war, a very real shooting battle involving rival gangs fighting to control hundreds of billions of dollars in product. And not only is the government unable to stop the war, in many cases, the government is part of it. To get the real story, journalist Gibler (*Mexico Unconquered*) hit the streets in some of the most dangerous Mexican cities and neighborhoods, speaking to reporters, photographers, kidnap victims, and the families of the murdered. The code of silence is difficult to break, since reporting on the drug cartels means almost certain death, often with impunity: only five percent of murders are investigated by the Mexican police. The problem is only growing, and the single thing likely to stop this juggernaut is drug legalization, which would make the trade less lucrative. But such a remedy isn't politic, and so the wars and the killings continue.

"Verdict: This grim but important chronicle is an essential read for anyone interested in the real consequences of the war-on-drugs rhetoric."

—*Library Journal*

"Gibler (*Mexico Unconquered*) documents Mexico's drug war, its enormous profits and grievous human costs, in taut prose and harrowing detail."

—*Publishers Weekly* (starred review)

"Gibler argues passionately to undercut this 'case study in failure.' The drug barons are only getting richer, the murders mount and the police and military repression expand as 'illegality increases the value of the commodity.' With legality, both U.S. and Mexican society could address real issues of substance abuse through education and public-health initiatives. A visceral, immediate and reasonable argument."

—*Kirkus*

"While these might be difficult pills to swallow, few will dispute the authority of Gibler's reporting or the force of his reasoning. For anyone still trying to make sense of it all, *To Die in Mexico* is a good place to begin."

—*San Antonio Express-News*

"What is groundbreaking about his book is his presentation in English of so many firsthand accounts that are typically available only in Spanish. News reports in the English-language media typically misrepresent Mexico as a 'drug nation' while keeping silent about the impact on victims and about who consumes the drugs. By presenting Mexican voices in English, Gibler allows us to see the dignity and humanity of those who are caught up in this tragic 'war.'"

—María Teresa Vázquez Castillo, *Aztlán:*
A Journal of Chicano Studies

"The historical context provided in *To Die in Mexico* is essential for understanding the current drug war in Mexico. Gibler covers the political, social, and economic factors that have contributed to the violence, convincingly making the case that 'absolute prohibition is legislated death.' Yet the true lifeblood of the book is the personal stories that Gibler tells through his interviews. Despite its title and thorough grounding in the disturbing reality of Mexico's narco-violence, *To Die in Mexico* is focused on life—the lives of Mexicans who have lost loved ones, the journalists who cover the drug war in spite of its dangers, and even the lives of the dead, who would otherwise remain anonymous."

—Anila Churi, *NACLA Report on the Americas*

WILMETTE PUBLIC LIBRARY

3 1239 00849 6041

ADVANCE PRAISE FOR *I COULDN'T EVEN IMAGINE
THAT THEY WOULD KILL US*

"Journalist Gibler (*To Die in Mexico*) delivers a meticulous and
affecting re-creation of the events of Sept. 26, 2014, in Iguala,
Mexico, when police attacked five buses carrying students from
the Ayotzinapa Teachers' College and a youth soccer team. Six
people died, 40 were wounded, and 43 students were loaded
into police trucks and never seen again. This powerful oral
history includes a chorus of voices: mainly the eyewitness accounts of the students but also the accounts of a teacher, soccer
officials, reporters at the scene, parents of 'the disappeared,'
and others. It begins with the students discussing the teachers'
college—why they chose it (for many, because it's free) and its
values of social action—and proceeds with an account of the
eight-hour attack and the aftermath in the school's basketball
court, where the families gathered between search expeditions.
Gibler, in his afterword, highlights how the scale of the tragedy
galvanized Mexico, a country where the drug war 'enabled these
forced disappearances,' and eventually led to an independent
investigation by a panel of international experts, the findings
of which contradict the government's story. It's a heartbreaking
reconstruction of a horrific event, made all the more profound
by the persistent demand from the parents of the disappeared,
their classmates, and citizens across country for the safe return
of the students."

—*Publishers Weekly* (starred review)

"In Mexico, John Gibler's book has been recognized as a jour-
nalistic masterpiece, an instant classic, and the most powerful
indictment available of the devastating state crime committed
against the 43 disappeared Ayotizinapa students in Iguala. This
meticulous, choral re-creation of the events of that night is bril-
liantly vivid and alive, it will terrify and inspire you and shatter
your heart."

—Francisco Goldman, author of *The Interior Circuit:
A Mexico City Chronicle*

WILMETTE PUBLIC LIBRARY
1242 WILMETTE AVENUE
WILMETTE, IL 60091
847-256-5025

"The hideous Ayotzinapa atrocity reveals with vivid horror how Mexico is being destroyed by the U.S.-based 'drug war' and its tentacles, penetrating deeply into the security system, business, and government, and strangling what is decent and hopeful in Mexican society. Gibler's remarkable investigations lift the veil from these terrible crimes and call for concerted action to extirpate the rotten roots and open the way for recovery from a grim fate."

—Noam Chomsky

"A powerful and searing account of a devastating atrocity. Gibler's innovative style takes us on a compelling journey through a landscape of terror and brutality against those whose only crime was to demand the freedom to think."

—Brad Evans is a columnist on violence for the *New York Times* and *LA Review of Books*

"We are fortunate to now have in English, John Gibler's courageous account and oral history of the 2014 atrocity in Mexico in which 43 students vanished from the face of the earth and remain absent, while six more people (three of them students) were found dead, one of them mutilated. The US 'war on drugs' has unleashed decades of unimaginable and hideous terrorism in Mexico, just as the 'war on terror' is doing in the Middle East. The cruel viciousness of Ayotzinapa, with the 48 families of all the disappeared, murdered, and critically wounded students insisting on answers from the Mexican government, opens the door to a powerful resistance movement, which also requires U.S. citizens to insist on ending the US war against the Mexican people, which began in the 1820s and has never abated."

—Roxanne Dunbar-Ortiz, author of *An Indigenous Peoples' History of the United States*

I Couldn't Even Imagine That They Would Kill Us

AN ORAL HISTORY OF THE ATTACKS
AGAINST THE STUDENTS OF AYOTZINAPA

John Gibler

Foreword by Ariel Dorfman

WITHDRAWN
Wilmette Public Library

WILMETTE PUBLIC LIBRARY

City Lights Books | San Francisco

Copyright © 2017 by John Gibler

Oral history translated from the Spanish by John Gibler

Foreword Copyright © 2017 by Ariel Dorfman

All Rights Reserved.

Open Media Series Editor: Greg Ruggiero

Cover illustration: © Owen Freeman/*California Sunday Magazine*
www.owenfreeman.com

Cover design: Herb Thornby

Maps: Jason Correia

Some portions of the afterword were originally published, in different
form, in the *California Sunday Magazine*.

ISBN: 978-0-87286-748-2
eISBN: 978-0-87286-749-9

Library of Congress Cataloging-in-Publication Data
on file

City Lights Books are published at the City Lights Bookstore
261 Columbus Avenue, San Francisco, CA 94133
www.citylights.com

364.
1523
GI

B.T 11/21/17

*For the survivors, the fallen, the disappeared
and their families.*

*And for all those who joined, and continue to
join, the struggle.*

Contents

How does one write a history of the impossible?
—Michel-Rolph Trouillot, *Silencing the Past: Power and the Production of History*

From whom can one demand justice if the same law that kills is the one that picks up the bodies? Where can one press charges if all the authorities are drenched in blood? The same law that takes measurements and conducts the investigation to discover who the killer is, is the one that committed the crime.
—Osiris in Alfredo Molano, *Desterrados: Crónicas del desarraigo*

Silence Is Not an Option

DESAPARECER.

That verb, in Spanish, had always been a passive one when I was growing up: *¿dónde desapareció mi libro?*, where did my book disappear to?, my mother or my father would wonder, trying to remember how that object could have been misplaced, who might have purloined or hidden it. *Desaparecer* was something that objects or people might do ("that cousin disappeared from our lives") but not an action perpetrated on those things, and certainly not something done to human beings. This simple usage—in Spanish as in other languages like English—had been customary for hundreds of years.

And then, suddenly, in late 1974, early 1975, there was a drastic change in the way that verb was implemented. My wife and I were in exile from Chile, wandering the world after the bloody coup d'état overthrew our democratically elected President Salvador Allende. It was in Paris that we began to hear *desaparecer* deployed actively: *lo desaparecieron, la desaparecieron*, they disappeared him or her or them. To disappear became a verb that described a crime, an act of violence committed against someone, something *done to* a living human being.

That new usage, that twist in the language, did not derive from an arbitrary pronouncement by some obscure member of the Academy of Letters or the faraway compiler of a dictionary. It was due to the need of ordinary people to express a terrifying form of repression that was being massively exercised by dictatorial governments of the Southern Cone of Latin America. Agents of the State were kidnapping opponents of the regime and then denying their relatives any knowledge about the men and women who had been arrested. The use of *desaparecer* in this new way arose from the determination to assign blame to those agents and that State, rather than allowing those violations to be covered up and obfuscated.

It was a response to a particularly cruel form of terror: those in power were trying to savagely eliminate anyone who showed the slightest sign of insubordination, and yet whitewash themselves of any responsibility for that persecution. The dictatorship wanted to spread fear everywhere (*Will I be next?*, *Will they take my son, my mother, my wife, my husband?*) and simultaneously claim there had been no abuse of human rights.

What these governments did not understand was that the families of the *desaparecidos*, primarily the mothers, were not going to let their *seres queridos* simply vanish into the darkness. The world witnessed how those relatives stood up to the authorities, demanding that those who had been detained be returned alive or, if they had been murdered, that their bodies be released so they might have a proper burial and commemoration. Anything but the uncertainty of not knowing the final fate of those missing sons and daughters, husbands and wives and parents. Emblematic of this resistance were the photos pinned to the dresses of women or held aloft on placards at rallies or silent marches.

Though such acts of defiance had their start in Chile and Argentina in the mid-1970s, they soon became globalized, as globalized as the terror they were protesting. Over the decades we were to see relatives from Afghanistan and Brazzaville and Myanmar adopt the same tactics; we witnessed how the missing of Ethiopia and Cyprus and Cambodia were all memorialized in this way.

And now it is Mexico, and the vicious abduction of the students of Ayotzinapa that has horrified our sad planet. Now it is the turn of Mexican fathers and mothers, brothers and friends of survivors, to make the disappeared *appear*, to make them *visible*, to keep them alive.

That struggle for truth has found a vibrant and respectful embodiment—yes, that is the right word—in John Gibler's heartrending, brave oral history of this collective fight against death, injustice, and oblivion.

Like the Mexican families who speak out in this book, he has refused to remain silent.

Precisely at a time when the United States is misgoverned by a belligerent bully who would like to make millions of Mexicans (not to mention other inhabitants of Latin American heritage) disappear from his country, precisely at a moment in history in which he and his followers dream of a gigantic wall separating these two bordering nations, this book propels us in another direction, jumping across those barriers with words that bring to the American public a tragedy that, if they are not careful, might someday violently touch their own lives.

Ayotzinapa is closer than you think.

—Ariel Dorfman, May 1, 2017
(*Día de los trabajadores*)

PROLOGUE

SOMETIME AROUND 9:00 P.M. on September 26, 2014, scores of uniformed police officers and a number of non-uniformed gunmen initiated a series of attacks against five buses of college students in Iguala, Guerrero, Mexico; a bus carrying a third-division, youth soccer team; and several cars and taxis driving on the highway about 15 kilometers outside of Iguala. The attacks took place, at times simultaneously in multiple locations, for over eight hours. Municipal, state, and federal police, along with civilian-clad gunmen, all collaborated that night to kill six people, seriously wound more than 40 (one of whom remains in a coma), and forcibly disappear 43 students from the Raúl Isidro Burgos Rural Teachers College in Ayotzinapa, Guerrero. The killers tortured, murdered, and cut off the face of one student, and then left his remains on a trash pile a few blocks from one of the scenes of attack.

From the beginning, the Guerrero state and Mexican federal governments lied about the attacks that took place that night in September. They minimized the significance of the disappearances and told stories of "confusion"—for example, that the "narcos" mistook the Ayotzinapa students for a rival drug gang. They tried, in various different ways, to blame the students for the violence they suffered. Federal authorities have propagated a soap opera–style depiction of a "corrupt" mayor and his "mafia" wife who ordered their "gangster" police to prevent the Ayotzinapa students from

17

protesting a political event that night, when in fact there was no such protest, nor even a plan to conduct such a protest. In reality, the students had no idea that said event was taking place, and the event concluded without the slightest interruption long before the students entered Iguala that night. Only a few days after the attacks, when it became clear that police had forcibly disappeared the 43 students, and upon observing the government's initial response (lies, rumors, trivializing the attacks, ignoring the parents), it also seemed clear that the government would do everything in its power to make it impossible to find the 43 students, and equally impossible to know what happened that night in Iguala. Almost three years later, as I write these words, the 43 families are still looking for their sons.

On October 3, 2014, I traveled from my room in Mexico City to Guerrero and spent most of the following nine months accompanying the families and students during their protests and mobilizations, interviewing survivors and witnesses of the attacks in Iguala. As the first anniversary of the attacks approached, I wanted to share the results of my reporting with the families of the disappeared, murdered, and wounded, with the many survivors of the attacks, as well as with those mobilizing alongside them across the country. I asked myself: How can I write about this? How can I best share what I have learned? What narrative form will best convey the stories that the survivors shared with me? And I thought to myself: This is not the time for me to write. What needs to be shared, urgently, are both the words and the storytelling of the people who lived through the attacks.

This book is composed with interviews with survivors of the attacks against the students of the the Raúl Isidro Burgos Rural Teachers College in Ayotzinapa during the night and predawn hours of September 26–27, 2014. I conducted the interviews between October 4, 2014, and June 19, 2015. The majority of survivors requested that I protect their identities with the use of pseudonyms; I have respected that request.

I have kept a few important words in Spanish. A *compañero* (or *compa*) is a companion in struggle and friend. A *paisa* (short for *paisano*) is a person from the same region or country, though the Ayotzinapa students also use it to refer to each other regardless of the region of the country they are from. A *campesino* is someone who lives in the countryside and works the land. A *zócalo* is a central plaza in a town or city. The students often use the words *tío* and *tía* (uncle and aunt) to refer in a respectful and tender way to adults. I have kept those words in Spanish when they are used in that way and translated them into English when the speaker is talking about an aunt or uncle.

Every year Ayotzinapa students elect a student governing committee with a secretary general and several sub-committees tasked with overseeing political organizing, cleaning, cooking and other activities. In what follows the students often refer to these various committees and to the "secretary" meaning the student governing committee's secretary general.

This book is an oral history of one night: a night of state terror. For the first edition, published in Mexico, in Spanish, in April 2016, I did not write an essay to accompany the oral history. I wanted my listening to act as accompaniment. I hoped that readers would do something similar: accompany, listen to the stories shared here, stories that describe a night of chaos and horror, erratic communications, confusion, shock and disbelief. For the English translation I have included this short prologue and an afterword providing some historical and political context on the region, the school, and the students' particular mode of organizing (including the "commandeering" of commercial buses, a practice mostly, if bitterly, tolerated by the bus companies and drivers), and discussion of the aftermath of the attacks, particularly the legal and administrative continuation of the atrocity.

Before the police attacks in Iguala, inspired by the Zapatista idea of "to lead by obeying" or *mandar obedeciendo*" and reflecting upon years of reporting on social struggles and state violence, I had begun to ask myself questions like these: What would it mean to write by listening, to *escribir escuchando*? What form would a writing that listens take? What would a politics of listening entail? I held these questions to myself as I began to work. The book you now hold in your hands is an attempt to write by listening.

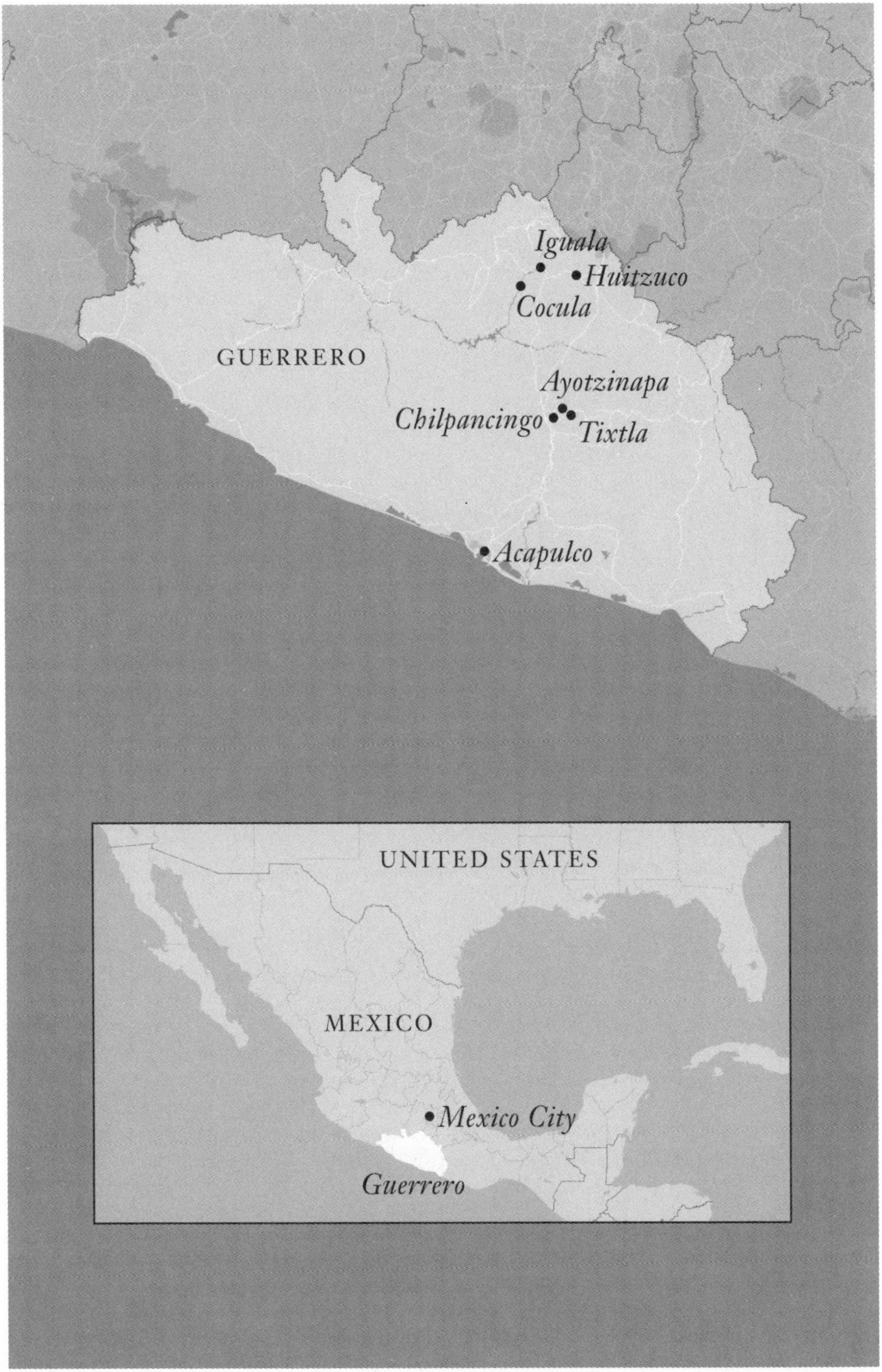
Iguala
Huitzuco
Cocula
GUERRERO
Ayotzinapa
Chilpancingo
Tixtla
Acapulco
UNITED STATES
MEXICO
Mexico City
Guerrero

• Intersection of Juan N. Álvarez & Periférico Norte

Iguala Central Plaza

Zona Militar

• Bus Station

Palacio de Justicia

IGUALA
GUERRERO, MEXICO

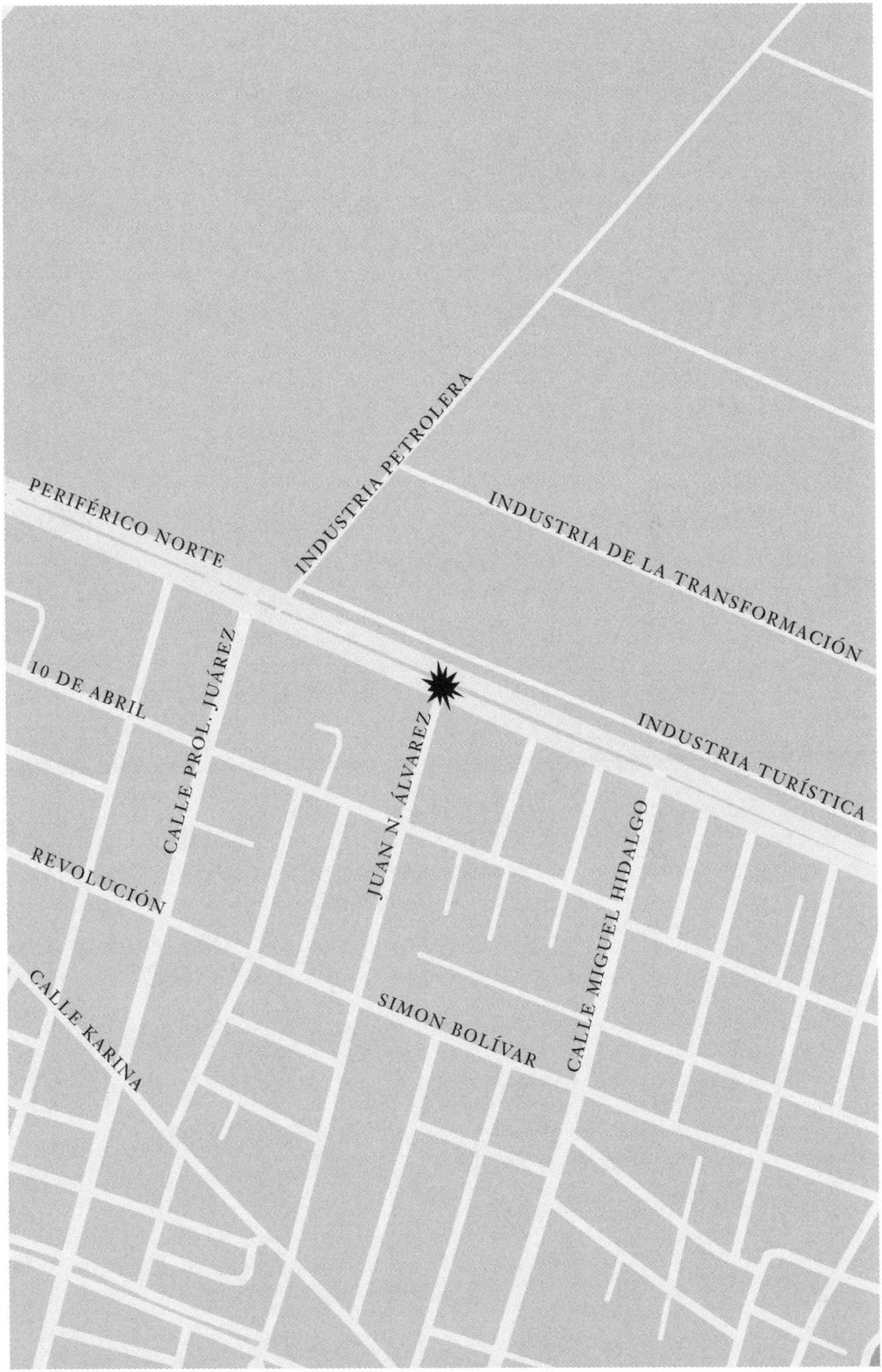
PERIFÉRICO NORTE
INDUSTRIA PETROLERA
INDUSTRIA DE LA TRANSFORMACIÓN
10 DE ABRIL
CALLE PROL. JUÁREZ
JUAN N. ÁLVAREZ
INDUSTRIA TURÍSTICA
CALLE MIGUEL HIDALGO
REVOLUCIÓN
SIMON BOLÍVAR
CALLE KARINA

IGUALA-CUERNAVACA
HEROICO COLEGIO MILITAR
MEXICAN FEDERAL HIGHWAY 95
Palacio de Justicia

An Oral History of Infamy

CARLOS MARTÍNEZ, 21, SOPHOMORE. I'm from a municipality in the region of the Costa Grande in Guerrero that is similar to Tixtla. It's a very pretty place, with rivers and lakes. Starting some time ago it began to urbanize, which has led to some problems. But even so, the essence of the place and the people remains. I'm the second of three siblings. I have an older sister and a younger sister. I am the middle child. I live with my mother. My father left years ago, so, it was really quite difficult to aspire to a different career.

I started working afternoons when I was in junior high school. I started working first at a mechanic's shop, then a hardware store, and then a taco stand. I did all that to try and support my studies, since it was hard on my mother, alone, having to provide for three kids. After much work, I was able to get a scholarship to study in Acapulco after finishing high school. I stayed there for a year studying accounting, but it was very expensive. I had to pay for inscription fees, books, rent, food, public transit, school projects, and all sorts of things. It was too much to cover with just the scholarship. After a while, I heard about the school here, Ayotzinapa, and I came here. I came hoping to be able to study, which is what I've always wanted.

I have a *compañero*, a friend who studied here and is now a teacher. I met him when I was working for a time in Atoyac de Álvarez. I met him there and he told me about this school, about it being a boarding school, about the classes, the cultural and athletic clubs, a bunch of things. But in the end what really grabbed my attention was that

27

the school is truly *free*: a school where you can really study and follow your path, that is free. That struck me, and that's why I came here.

SANTIAGO FLORES, 24, FRESHMAN. Many of my friends said that we should all go to study in Acapulco or at the college for physical education teachers in Michoacán. But I wasn't really into that idea because it's hard for me to be far from home. A cousin of mine graduated from here and said that I should come here, that all the expenses are covered—the school covers everything—and for that reason, really, the economics, that's why I came.

JORGE HERNÁNDEZ ESPINOSA, 20, FRESHMAN. My brother graduated from the college here in 2011. He came in 2007 without knowing anything about this place or what he was getting into. He had heard that there is a teachers college, a boarding college, near Chilpancingo, it's called Ayotzinapa; all you have to do is take an exam, pass it, and pass a trial week and that's it. That's all he knew, so he arrived here without a clue. He passed the trial week, and he graduated. He told me: "I want you to go study there."

To begin with, we didn't have money. My father had abandoned us. We are five children, four brothers and one sister. My brother was in his last year [at the college] when my father left us. My mother took care of us. One of my brothers and my sister were in high school with me. One of my brothers was in junior high, and my other brother is both hearing- and speech-impaired and wasn't in school. So my older brother graduated from Ayotzinapa.

"If you want to study," he said to me, "you don't really

have a choice, go there, you'll learn a lot." And he explained to me more or less how things operate at the college.

"Sure, I'll go," I said to him. I didn't think twice about it. I arrived here at the college and in all honesty I felt strange, uncomfortable for having left my family. I wasn't used to leaving my house for any length of time. I didn't know anyone at the school. I arrived without knowing anything or anyone. I said to myself, "This is so I can get ahead," so that one day my family can say, "I'm proud of you for what you have achieved. Big or small, what you have achieved is important."

JUAN PÉREZ, 25, FRESHMAN. The majority of students here are the sons of *campesinos*. Where I come from we only have an elementary school, a middle school, and a high school. We don't have any other options for study or pursuing a career, my small town is a bit more fucked-over than other places. I decided to come to this school, to study, to be someone, to go back to my town and be a teacher there, and give classes to the kids. Since in my town we all speak Me'phaa, we want a teacher who speaks Me'phaa. That's the vision I have for myself.

COYUCO BARRIENTOS, 21, FRESHMAN. My father separated from my mother when I was about five years old. We lived in the mountains. But my mom, my sister, and I went to live with my grandparents then, nearer to the town center. My mom would leave us to go to work. We would stay with my grandmother, because my grandfather worked all day too, coming back at night, or if not, at the end of the week. So I became quite independent. By the time I came here, I wasn't speaking to my father, it had been some time since we fought. Before coming here I had thought about joining the marines to pay for my studies and support my family. But it didn't work out. I was almost accepted and at that point didn't have any other options. I had studied tourism in Acapulco, but without any support. Around that time I had fought with my mom and my sister and was on my own. I had to work. I stopped studying and my cousin told me that if I wanted, I should come study here, that there was nothing else that could help me.

And so this became . . . like a light of hope, because I wanted to keep studying. I didn't want to get stuck just working, so I took his advice. And it turned out that my cousin—he's from Zihuatanejo, Daniel Solís—also was going to come take the entrance exam. So we arranged to meet up and we came. Before that, I took any job I could find. I helped my uncles to repair and clean refrigerators, washing machines, air conditioners. I made very little, but enough to get by. After that I went to look for more work and found an automobile body and paint shop. I showed up there knowing nothing, but started to learn just by watching. I got the hang of it quickly. The boss began to trust me and to give me jobs, simple ones that I could handle. And I told him that I needed to work to put together enough money to come and take the entrance exam. I needed to pay the travel costs and have something for whatever I'd need here. He understood and gave me a hand. I worked with him for about a month and a half, up until the day when I had to come here.

ANDRÉS HERNÁNDEZ, 21, FRESHMAN. I have a goal, which is to become a teacher, an educator. I came here with that objective, to go back and give classes in my community, which is quite remote, a community of about 200 people. The teachers who sometimes go there, I don't know if it's because of the heat or the food, but they leave after only a little while. They don't even last half a year before requesting a change. That's why I came here. I'm here with that goal: to be able to go back to my community and give classes, to be an educator there.

EDGAR ANDRÉS VARGAS, 20, JUNIOR. When we were in our third year of high school a number of kids started talking about where they wanted to study. The only teachers college that we had heard of was Tenería, in the State of Mexico. But my cousin, Óliver, told me that there was a teachers college like Tenería in Guerrero. But to tell you the truth, I was never inspired to go to a teachers college. My cousin told me that his uncle studied at the teachers college in Guerrero and that it was good. So he said we should go, he was trying to convince me, but I didn't really want to, in all honesty. He went to the school to begin the admissions process and told me all about it, that I should apply as well. On the very last day I made up my mind. I left my town around two in the morning. I went with my father, because the school is quite far away. My cousin told me more or less how to get there.

I started the admissions process on the last day. I was one of the very last to apply. I walked around the college and I started to like it. I'm really close to my cousin; we've been friends since elementary school and we were excited to take the exam. Once I saw the place, the murals and everything, I was more interested and decided to take the exam.

JOSÉ ARMANDO, 20, FRESHMAN. This is the reason we come study at Ayotzinapa: because we are the sons of *campesinos*. We don't have the resources to study at another school. And this school is committed to social struggle; it's a school where we learn the values to keep fighting and create a better future, to support our families. And what does the government do? It kills students.

MIGUEL ALCOCER, 20, FRESHMAN. I came, really, due to a lack of money. I stopped studying for two years for that same reason: I didn't have any money. I wanted to keep studying but my parents didn't have more money to give me and there weren't any savings. I already knew about this school and wanted to come, but it wasn't until 2014 that I made up my mind. So I told my parents that I was going to come, and they said okay. You know, it was the only option, economically, because here you don't pay anything for food or lodging. Here the school provides everything, and that's why I wanted to come here.

JORGE HERNÁNDEZ ESPINOSA, 20, FRESHMAN. At the beginning, during the trial week, honestly, we didn't like it. We asked ourselves: "Why do they do this to us if we just want to study?" But truthfully, during that experience you start to value certain things. You learn to appreciate everything from your family, meals, your *compañeros*, your friends, everything, everything. Because you hit a point where you get tired and say to yourself, "I can't do this anymore; I'm going home." But then you say, "I'll get home and what will I tell my parents? Here I am, I couldn't do it; I gave up, I couldn't pass the trial week?" And that's how you find courage inside yourself, and you think about your family and think: "I don't want to let my family down; I want to make them proud; I want to go home and be able to tell them: I made it."

It's really true, the trial week is hard. We work; they make us do all the work of a *campesino*, because we are *campesinos*. But, for example, the work that a *campesino* does in a month, we do that in a week. We multiply the work.

There are times when we don't drink water, when we don't eat. It's true and it's hard. But at the same time, once you've been there at the college for two or three days during the trial week, you say to yourself: "I made it two days, just five more to go. I'm going to stick it out." And you do.

SANTIAGO FLORES, 24, FRESHMAN. The trial week is tough. It was really kind of grueling. But, you know, that's how it is here, that's how they do it every year. They have you doing exercise, doing farm work, clearing brush and weeds from the fields, going out to help *los tíos* in their fields. It's pretty exhausting, and only those who make it through the trial week get admitted. We helped each other out, though. If some of us couldn't run anymore, the organizers would encourage us.

"Help each other out," they would say, "help each other; never leave a *compa* alone, no one should ever get left behind; when you're finished running, there should be no one left behind."

If one of us couldn't go on, we all had to stop and wait, or try to help him out by carrying him, but no one could be left on their own. That's where we start building a sense of being *compañeros* within the group, always staying together, never leaving anyone behind, helping each other out. That's where the *compañerismo* begins. We make deep friendships during the trial week. We become best friends during that experience with *compañeros* we didn't know before.

EDGAR ANDRÉS VARGAS, 20, JUNIOR. On the first day they took us all into the auditorium. The students from the committee welcomed us, more or less, told us some stuff and then let us out early. We went to rest. Around four in the morning some of the students from the sports club showed up kicking our doors, shouting. In that situation, you wake up in a flash. They told us to be out on the soccer field in five minutes, or like two minutes. Since we had heard a bit about the trial week, we had an idea of what was about to happen. They made us do exercises and then run. They took us running. This was kind of complicated for me since I used to have asthma and always used an inhaler. I still was afraid I'd have an asthma attack, that's why I hardly ever played soccer anymore. But in that moment we all took off running. And they had us chanting. Truth be told, it was tiring running up stairs, doing all that exercise, I wasn't really used to all that. They made us run all through Tixtla. We went almost as far as the OXXO convenience store at the edge of town, and then they brought us back, running. They gave us a few minutes to rest and then, around eight or nine, they took us out to do shifts as lookouts, to sweep the school grounds, to clear weeds with a machete and all that.

The hard thing was that they didn't give us any water to drink. There was very little water, and they didn't give us water to drink. So, to be out there cutting weeds with a machete, thirsty, you get exhausted. But I didn't give up. And then the meals were just some tortillas and a tiny spoonful of beans. Tough luck. You were hungry and you had to eat it and you couldn't ask for more, because if you did they would fill every inch of your plate with beans, they'd give you bread and tortillas, but a lot of them, and you had to eat it all. So you had to settle for what they gave you. I think they gave us breakfast around ten or eleven and then a few minutes to rest, and then back to work: work, work, work. Then it wasn't until around four or five that they fed us again. And those were the only two meals. They talked to us about the college, about its creation and everything, and then around eight at night they took us to the study groups and gave us political orientation. They talked about the essence of the teachers colleges, the founding of the teachers colleges, about the social movements there have been in the country, and about the bad governments.

Sometimes they showed us videos, films, but always related to, you could say, left politics. We would get out of there really late, around two or three in the morning. I remember that twice they took me out of the movies because I had fallen asleep. That was during the last days of the trial week. The students' committee took me out of the movie because I had fallen asleep and they made me do exercises there in front of the auditorium. The first time they made me exercise, they told me to climb up all these stairs to see what was written on a cross. It was night. I didn't go all the way, because I saw another guy coming down, I think they sent him up there to do the same thing, and so I just asked him what was written on the cross and then we sat there talking for a bit. Then we went back and they asked us what was written on the cross, we told them, and they sent us back into the auditorium until the study group was over.

The other time they took me out was also because I had fallen asleep; I was so tired I just couldn't stay awake. But that time they made me eat an onion. They asked you if you wanted an apple or a pear. I remember that I said an apple and the apple was an onion, the pear was a habanero chili pepper. I chose the apple. And they told me I had to eat it, and I ate it. Afterward I couldn't sleep. The smell was everywhere. It made your eyes cry. I had that taste in my mouth for three or four days.

And I made my way through the trial week. It was tough. A bunch of applicants couldn't take the exhaustion or the hunger, and they left. Once they took us out to cut all the weeds from the cornfields. We went in a bus and got off on the shoulder of the highway and had to climb up the mountain. We arrived around noon I think, and in the sun began to cut the weeds. By around two, I couldn't stand the thirst. I was so thirsty, my whole body felt weak. When I went to the trial week I didn't take anything, just a couple of changes of clothes and a backpack. I didn't take a blanket, just a towel. At night it would get cold and what I would do was lay out a change of clothes on the floor—the concrete floor would get really cold—and I'd lie down and cover myself with the towel. But after a while I struck up a friendship with the guy next to me: he had brought sheets and he shared his mattress with me.

I made it through a lot. It was kind of messed up, because they would take us out to clear weeds when it was raining, with thunder, and they wouldn't let us take cover. The trial week was tough, but I was able to make it through.

ÓSCAR LÓPEZ HERNÁNDEZ, 18, FRESHMAN. In all honesty, they treated us pretty badly when we showed up here that first week. But even so, with what happened to us on the twenty-sixth, it all was useful. Here at the college, during trial week, they have us run, jump into the pool early in the morning, and that came in handy for real, because on the night of the twenty-sixth with the rain, me and several other *compañeros* spent some eight hours wet. And, yes, here at the college they do that to us, they make us jump in the pool and then go running all wet, and do exercise in the morning. And seriously, on that day, everything they had done to us during the trial week was really fucking useful because out there you really needed it, you had no idea where to run, and here at the college they had taught us to run and seek shelter, and to be in shape.

MIGUEL ALCOCER, 20, FRESHMAN. It's a week when you're here and you go out and do all the things that a *campesino* does: clear the weeds with a machete, feed the livestock, plant, feed the pigs and the hens. All that is what we do during adjustment week, as they also call it, to see if we are really the sons of *campesinos*. The truth is, for me it was easy because it was all things I've done with my parents. We've worked the land, we have some land and livestock. For me, I didn't think it was hard because, you know, it's stuff I do at home with my parents and my brother.

CARLOS MARTÍNEZ, 21, SOPHOMORE. I had finished my freshman year and was eager to start classes and keep studying. We even had plans in my sophomore class to take a study trip; we were planning on going to Chiapas. I felt a bit more relaxed, because the freshman year here is really intense. You show up and you have to adapt to life here at the school, to the academics, the way of life here, the context, the government harassment and persecution that's always present, I mean it never dissipates, and you have to start, little by little, getting used to the idea that this school isn't just any school, this school is very different.

When I was a freshman there was a flood here in Tixtla. This whole area down here flooded. Just about half of the municipality of Tixtla flooded. Many people lost everything: their houses, their belongings, and their work. The rains started on September 13, I still recall that day well, and it kept raining without a break for several days. All of Tixtla flooded, and almost immediately a bunch of people came here to ask us for help getting their things, their belongings out of their houses. There were sick people who couldn't walk, the elderly, and they needed our help. And there we went when I was a freshman, in September, with the rains, with the water up to our necks, taking things out of the houses and cars, and helping people with any number of things. And that was where they taught us not only to look out for ourselves, but for everyone. It was a fast reaction. I'll admit that maybe it wasn't organized, but it did meet the need of helping the people of Tixtla out.

Later, the federal government designated all sorts of resources, hundreds of thousands of pesos to help this area recover. And to this day, many of the people affected haven't received a thing. In fact, one time the army made a video where they paid some people to pretend to be wounded or something, and the soldiers were carrying them in the water. And they splashed water on their faces... well, they were actors, they were basically actors for the army. And the people here were so outraged when they saw that the only thing the army had come to do was pretend, precisely when people needed help. Because the soldiers didn't get in the water, they didn't go into the flooded houses to remove people's things. They didn't go in the water to rescue people. We did that. And the people were so out-raged when they found out that the army was making that video that they went out to where the soldiers were, they encircled the soldiers and wouldn't let them leave until they made a public apology.

I was also there on January 7, when two *compañeros* were run over in Atoyac de Álvarez. It was an accident, a hit and run. We were out [on the roadside] asking for donations, when a truck pulling some kind of heavy machinery—I don't know what it's called, maybe an excavator, it had like a shovel on it—and even though we were out in the road, the truck came through really fast and some *compañeros* weren't able to move fast enough, to get out of the road. Three *compañeros* made it out alive, two others died there. Eugenio Tamari Huerta and Freddy Fernando Vázquez Crispín were the two who died there. We went after the person who had crashed into the *compañeros*. We followed him and were able to capture him about three towns down the highway, a place called El Cayaco. We held him there until the police arrived and took him away. That guy is in prison now for the murder of the two *compañeros*.

At times it might seem that you live through more bad experiences here than good, but that's not true.

ERICK SANTIAGO LÓPEZ, 22, SOPHOMORE. It was around six in the evening when we gathered everyone together. The action that we had planned for that evening was to get some buses, nothing else. We left the school in two buses from the Estrella de Oro line. The action was planned in that moment, but long before that we had had a meeting with the student federation from the seventeen rural teachers colleges. In that meeting we planned for the

October 2 march in Mexico City.[1] Here at my school, as always, we try to support the other teachers colleges. So with the secretary and the other members of the committee—and at that time, I was a member of the committee—we came to an agreement that we would round up about twenty-five buses to transport our *compañeros* and *compañeras* from the other colleges. This had already been planned, but only people within the committee knew about it. Only the committee knows about the plans when we agree on actions, the student rank and file doesn't know about the plans. We decided to head out that afternoon and make a call to the students that only the freshman would be going out on an action. We always take the freshman out on the actions, not the sophomores. Why? Because here at our college we say that the freshmen have to take the lead. After them, the sophomores, and at the back the seniors. Why? Because they are the ones who have to spearhead the activities. And the members of the committee go in front with the freshmen. The committee also goes at the lead, and everyone else behind them.

JOSÉ LUIS GARCÍA, 20, FRESHMAN. On the twenty-sixth of September we were out working in the fields. They called us together because we'd be going out on an action

---

1. On October 2, 1968, on the eve of the Olympic games to be held in Mexico City, Mexican President Gustavo Díaz Ordaz ordered the army to crush the student protest movement. Soldiers ambushed and massacred hundreds of students during a protest in the Tlatelolco Plaza in Mexico City. The government denied that the massacre had taken place, called it a "confrontation," disappeared many of the dead, and conducted mass arrests of student leaders. The massacre left a profound mark on Mexican society and is commemorated every year with a large march from Tlatelolco to the Zócalo in Mexico City.

to collect donations. And so we all got on the buses. It was around five or five-thirty in the afternoon. We went to our rooms to get T-shirts and then we left.

OMAR GARCÍA, 24, SOPHOMORE. On the morning of the twenty-sixth we tried to go to Chilpancingo, but we couldn't get any buses there. The police stopped us. And, you know, that's fine, no? They stopped us as they should stop us, without beatings, without anything like that, strictly following protocol. And so we left empty-handed.

"Where are we going to go now," we wondered, "what are we going to do? We absolutely have to have two more buses by this afternoon. If not, we're not going to make the goal."

COYUCO BARRIENTOS, 21, FRESHMAN. The argument I had with my mom had happened around January. Since then I had not communicated with her. On the afternoon of September 26, while we were in marching band practice, I saw, off in the distance, that she—my mom—was arriving. I stepped away from the *compañeros*, asked permission, and the vice principal gave me a chance to go talk with her. I hadn't told her, in fact I had told hardly anyone, that I would be coming to study here. I had just focused on working, saving some money, and no one knew. I went and spoke with my mom, and after so much time you feel . . . well, nostalgia. All the other *compañeros*' moms, or at least some relative of theirs, would come to visit them or send them something, money, or even just call them. And there I was, alone, without anyone to call me, or make some gesture of caring, or anything. To be honest, it was intense; I never imagined, after so much time, that she would come out here. Afterward, with band practice over, I went to my room to rest. That was when I started to notice that there was something going on. They started to call us, to tell us that we should get ready, that we would be going out to an action. We started to gather together and head toward the bus. The majority of us didn't know what action we would be going on. They just said: "Let's go, this way." Later they told us: "We're going to Iguala to ask for donations." And so we all took our seats, we were relaxed.

Other *compañeros* hadn't had a chance to leave the school grounds. It was the first time they were going out. Some were talking, others were joking around. Others of us were quiet. In fact, for some groups that had been the first day of classes. And personally, for me, after not having seen my mom for so much time, it was the very day that she had come here, precisely that day. On the road I felt a kind of heavy vibe. Everything was calm. But I sensed something strange. But, you know, we kept going.

JOSÉ ARMANDO, 20, FRESHMAN. We had our first class that morning. We all got up excited that morning: we were happy, joking around with each other. We had class, went to eat lunch, and then went to another class. They called us out to the *módulos*, which is doing farm work in the different fields on campus. We went and were working in the fields, planting corn and *cempasúchil* and *tapayola* flowers. And there we were, clearing the cornfields, everyone in a good mood. Who could have imagined what was about to happen? At five o'clock they called us to go out on an action. The plan wasn't to go to Iguala. We were going to get some buses for a reason, because Ayotzinapa was to host other students who would all travel together to the October 2 march that's held every year to commemorate the Massacre of Tlatelolco. And so we went. We left from here at six. We all gathered together and we went in two buses that we already had at the school, they were from the company Estrella de Oro. And we went, everyone in a good mood, like we always are when we go out to an action, laughing, wrestling, and so on.

GERMÁN, 19, FRESHMAN. We were working in the fields that we have here when some of our *compañeros* came up and said, "*Compas*, we're heading out for an action, everyone get ready." We went off happy, running. We stopped the fieldwork and left. We got on the bus. I was with one of my *compañeros* who is disappeared. (In fact, five of the *compañeros* that are now disappeared are my friends.) So, with all of them we were messing around like always, you see how we are, talking, fucking around, talking about girls, everything.

SANTIAGO FLORES, 24, FRESHMAN. They had told us that that day in the afternoon they would let us go, we could leave the campus, I think for five days. They sent us to do fieldwork. They sent us to cut the weeds that had grown up in the cornfields. In the afternoon we were clearing the weeds, we were joking around with each other. The *compa* in charge had told us that as soon as we finished we'd be able to go home for a few days of vacation. But then some other *compas* from the committee showed up and told us that there would be an action. They told us we had to go, that it was required.

With another *compa* I went from the fields to change, we went to get a jacket, or a sweater, since it was already late afternoon and we thought we'd be out after nightfall. My *compañero* didn't want to go. He is disappeared. His name is Jesús Jovany Rodríguez Tlatempa. We call him *El Churro*, Doughnut. He told me he didn't want to go. I don't know if he sensed something, but he didn't want to go. I told him that we should go, because if not we'd get punished. And so he said to me: "Okay, let's go."

ALEX ROJAS, FRESHMAN. On September 26, we were at dance club practice when they told us there was going to be an action. They didn't tell us exactly what kind of action it would be. And so, around six in the afternoon, together with the other *compañeros* from the dance club and other clubs, we went to the parking lot to get on one of the two Estrella de Oro buses. We got on the buses. I was in the second bus. We were all talking and having a good time. During the trip I was seated next to a *compañero* who was one of my better friends at the school. He's from the town of Apango. And we were talking about how we wouldn't get separated, we would stick together. I said that whatever happened we'd try and return early. We had heard that we were going to get two or three buses to use to drive to the October 2 march commemorating the massacre of students at Tlatelolco. And so we agreed that if we were going to hijack buses, we'd get on the first bus we grabbed, so we could get back to school early and avoid any trouble. My *compañero*, the one who was sitting next to me, is named Miguel Ángel Mendoza. He is disappeared.

ANDRÉS HERNÁNDEZ, 21, FRESHMAN. That afternoon I—I'm in the dance club—I had finished dance practice. We finished practice and went back to our rooms. Then they called us, saying that there was going to be an action. And so, you know, we went.

CARLOS MARTÍNEZ, 21, SOPHOMORE. Every year people commemorate the October 2 massacre in Mexico City. A whole lot of organizations from the Federal District and beyond all participate. A part of the commitment that we make to attend the march is to gather enough buses to get to the march. The issue here is that we have spent so much time asking the state government for buses to be able to get around. For example, during the week of September 22 to 25, we went to conduct classroom observations in a place called Copala, in the Costa Chica region of Guerrero.

When you go to do classroom observations, there are two options: you pay your way, or you figure something else out, because the state doesn't provide travel expenses, lodging, or food. In other words, they make it a requirement for you to go out there and that's it. Our observations took place during the week of the twenty-second to the twenty-fifth, but the freshmen observations were coming up, and that's why they had to go out on the action, it's a tradition. If juniors have to go to classroom observations, then they have to get the buses. If those who are going to do observations are sophomores, then the sophomores have to get their buses. If the *compañeros* who are going to do classroom exercises or observations are freshmen, then they go for the buses. So our plan was to get buses for the October 2 march and the upcoming freshmen observations.

We got back to school from our observations on the

night of the twenty-fifth. I was really tired and went to sleep. I got up on the twenty-sixth and went to Chilpancingo to shop for some things and returned to the school around three or four in the afternoon. I was coming down the stairs and ran into Bernardo, the sophomore *compañero* who's disappeared. I ran into Bernardo and he told me to go with them. I told him I had a whole bunch of stuff to do: I had to write a report, a paper we have to write when we go out to do classroom exercises. But he told me to go with them, that it would only be a while, it would be quick, and we'd have Saturday and Sunday to do our schoolwork.

"Okay then," I said, "let's go."

We left from the college parking lot around five, maybe, around five o'clock. It took a while, a really long time, to get to Iguala, because there was construction on the highway and we were stuck there for maybe an hour and a half. We were there for a good while waiting for them to finish and open the road. We were all in good moods. The freshmen were all making jokes, messing around with each other. No one imagined that what happened was going to happen. When we got to Iguala we veered off the main highway and split up. We were in two Estrella de Oro buses. One bus stayed in Huitzuco to ask for donations, and the other bus, where I was riding, went to the Iguala tollbooth. When we got there it was beginning to get dark. The plan was to stay there and grab a bus.

ÓSCAR LÓPEZ HERNÁNDEZ, 18, FRESHMAN. That day, September 26, we were out working, like always. We work in the afternoons and that day the committee members came and said: "*Paisas, ¡jálense!* Everybody get over here! Action! We're going to get some buses!"

MIGUEL ALCOCER, 20, FRESHMAN. That day, the twenty-sixth, we woke up early and went to the dining hall for breakfast at seven, I think. After that we had classes. We went to class. After that the teachers gave us homework. Here at the school there are five areas: farm work, academics, marching band, the *rondalla* [a guitar-based song group], and dance. After classes we had dance practice. We rehearsed and then got out at five. We went to the dining hall again, and since they had told us that we would be going to observe what a teacher does in the classroom, we wanted two buses, because we didn't have other transportation. We left here around six, on the way to Iguala, to get the buses we need to go do classroom observations.

URIEL ALONSO SOLÍS, 19, SOPHOMORE. On September 26, I remember, we sophomores had gone to observe elementary schools in the Costa Chica. I remember those days in the communities well. I came back to school on the twenty-sixth at around three in the afternoon. The *compa* in charge of organizing that action, a sophomore, is disappeared. His name is Bernardo Flores, but we call him *Cochiloco*, Crazy Pig. He told me that there would be an action in the afternoon. And to be honest, I felt like staying at the school. I had a bad feeling that something was going to happen.

The first thing that came to mind was that we'd surely clash with riot police. But I recalled that we sophomores always have to be on the front lines when things come to blows, running alongside the freshmen. We got on the two Estrella de Oro buses here at the school and left for Iguala. We didn't go to Chilpancingo because in previous days we had clashed with the police there. So we decided not to go there, thinking that surely there would be a lot of cops there to beat us back. We left here around six.

During the drive everything was really fun. We were all playing, joking around with the bus drivers. We cranked the music as loud as it would go. It was all fun, play, joy, and laughter.

IVÁN CISNEROS, 19, SOPHOMORE. That day the *compañero* who was president of the Struggle Committee here at the college had asked me to help him coordinate an action. I said yes because we had just returned from our classroom observations the day before. But I told him that we should make it quick, because I needed to write my report because the teachers wanted it on Monday. I remember well that I told him yes.

"We leave at five," he told me.

"Ah, okay," I said, "that's fine." Afterwards I went to my room. A few minutes before five I ran into the Struggle Secretary, the one we called *Cochi*, a *compañero* who is disappeared, named Bernardo, also a sophomore.

"Hey, *paisa*, we're going to the action," he said, "we're going to bring back some buses."

"Sure thing," I said, "let's go." So I went to let some other *compañeros* from the Order Committee know. There I asked the president, I said:

"Hey man, what's up? Aren't you coming?"

"Help me out, no? I've got to make a trip to Chilpo. Cover for me."

"Sure, man. No worries."

We kept walking and *Cochi* said to me:

"*Compa*, I need more people. We're going to get some buses."

"Okay, no problem."

"Lend me the activists."

"That's not my decision. That's up to the COPI,[2]"—and right there was the *compa* in charge of the COPI and *Cochi* asked him.

"Hey, lend me the activists so we can go bring some buses."

The COPI asked me directly:

"Are you going?"

"Yeah, I'm going," I told him.

"Alright then, take 'em."

And so the activists came out and got on the bus.

The atmosphere on the bus was fucking cool, for real. We were joking around. We were on two buses, two Estrellas de Oro. I was riding with the driver that everyone called *Chavelote*, Big Kid, and behind us, in the other bus, there were two other bus drivers. One was called *Ambulancia*, Ambulance, and the other *Manotas*, Big Hands. *Manotas* was driving the bus and *Ambulancia* was just going along for the ride. The atmosphere, I tell you, was fucking awesome. The freshmen were all joking around, and those of us sophomores at the front of the bus were doing the same.

The ones who were riding with *Manotas* and *Ambulancia* stayed behind at a place called Rancho del Cura, to ask for donations, and we went to the highway to grab the buses. We stopped and were just waiting for some buses to drive by so we could grab them. But there we noticed something strange. When some buses started to approach on the highway, the federal police stopped the buses, made the passengers get off, and sent the buses back. And the passengers came from the tollbooth on foot.

---

2. Comité de Organización Política e Ideológica (Political and Ideological Organizing Committee).

That's when I said to *Cochi*: "No, man, the jig is up, we aren't going to be able to grab anything." We were going to go back to the college when we got a call that some other *compañeros*, who had grabbed a bus that was going to drop its passengers off at the station, were being detained. So we took off fast, we went straight to the bus station to bust out the *compañeros* being held there.

ÓSCAR LÓPEZ HERNÁNDEZ, 18, FRESHMAN. There in Huitzuco we started to keep a look out for buses. First we grabbed a Costa Line. Right then we asked the driver to take us to the college, because we were going to go to an event on October 2, the march they hold every year. And yes, the driver said, okay, and ten *compañeros* got on the bus because first the driver was going to drop off the passengers in Iguala. Ten *compañeros* got on the bus. About ten minutes went by and they hadn't come back, so the guy from the committee said to call those *compañeros*, because a lot of time had passed. We tried to reach the *compañeros*. Then one of them called us and said: "*Compas*, we've got a problem here with security, the bus driver won't let us out, he locked us in the bus."

URIEL ALONSO SOLÍS, 19, SOPHOMORE. First we went to the Huitzuco stop and the first bus arrived. We spoke with the driver and he said yes. There were about five of us who got on the bus. We arrived at the bus station and that's when he said, "No, can't do it, nope. . . ." He had changed his mind and said no, not anymore. And since we were already there and we didn't have any money with us to get back, we called the *compañeros*.

"You know what, come get us," we said. "We're in the bus station. The driver changed his mind. We're trapped on board the bus, the driver already got off. He locked us in."

"Hold tight," they said, "we're on our way." And that's when they came.

EDGAR YAIR, 18, FRESHMAN. We left around five-thirty, I think. We left in two buses from the parking lot here. I was in the second bus. The bus was sort of packed, there were a bunch of us. We arrived at the entrance to Iguala. We got out where we were going to do the action. It was around six or seven at night. Around eight o'clock a bus drove by. The driver was going to help us out, you know, getting to the march. But he had passengers. So the driver needed to drop off his passengers at their destination, which was the bus station in Iguala.

Ten of our *compañeros*, about ten, got on the bus. They left with the bus and we stayed back in the same place where we'd been. Well, we'd been out there for about another hour and we saw that our *compañeros* didn't return. It was night at that point, it was already dark. Then we got a call from a *compañero* who said they'd been held at the bus station. We had to go and set them free. So we went. We got there and we all covered our faces with our T-shirts, so they couldn't identify us, to protect our identities. We were there demanding that they let our *compañeros* out. At last they let them go, but we were angry by that point, and we grabbed three buses from the station there. We forced the drivers to take us in the buses. Two buses went a different way out of the station and the other three buses went out toward Avenue Juan N. Álvarez.

ALEX ROJAS, FRESHMAN. The two buses stopped near Huitzuco along a part of the highway that's really straight. There's a restaurant near there; I think it's called La Palma. We stopped there by the restaurant. There's a little chapel there where a number of us who are believers went to pray and make the sign of the cross. The first bus left. I don't know exactly where it went, but it took off toward Iguala and I think they went to the tollbooth. I think they were going to do the action there. We stayed there, near the restaurant, where the highway is really straight, to avoid any accidents.

We started to do the action, and sure enough, a bus passed by, which we stopped and commandeered. The bus had passengers on board. So as not to affect the bus riders, we decided to take them to the station. I got on that bus with another seven *compañeros* and a member of the committee. We boarded the bus and left. I was talking with some of the passengers on their way to Iguala. They said to me that they were afraid and asked us not to do anything to them. I told them not to worry, that we never did anything to citizens, to the people, that we only did this action because it was necessary since we don't have any vehicles at the school to use for transportation to our actions, whether it's going to the march to commemorate the student massacre, or fundraising activities, or the classroom observations and exercises that the sophomores, juniors, and seniors all do.

I was talking with a woman and some other people in that part of the bus, telling them not to worry, that we never mean to inconvenience them, much less harm them, that we were just kids who were at the college to study, but that it was necessary to do this to be able to carry out our activities and attend some events at the other rural teachers colleges. That's what I was talking with them about. A number of passengers were talking with us, and we were all getting along well.

"Yes, guys, we understand, but we still got scared when you all stopped the bus."

"Don't worry," I said to them, "we're going to the bus station, we'll let you all off there without any problems and we'll then continue with our action like we do every year, totally normal."

We arrived at the bus station and yeah, all the passengers got off. We stayed on board the bus and told the driver that we had to get back. The driver agreed and asked us to wait a moment. But after about fifteen minutes, we got nervous that he wouldn't want to come back. We told him:

"Let's go now, driver!"

But the driver said no, that he had to get authorization, and well, he was just stalling. That's when we called our *compañeros* so they would come help us. We were just eight kids, with the guy from the committee, nine, I think. So we called the ones who were out on the fundraising action.

ERICK SANTIAGO LÓPEZ, 22, SOPHOMORE. During that time a number of strange things started to happen. We were already out by the Iguala tollbooth. A red motorcycle started driving by. And a bit later a Policía Federal truck passed. . . . That truck went through the tollbooth to the other side and started to stop all the buses. The police started to make the passengers get off of all the buses that arrived—Estrella, Futura, Costa Line, Diamante, any bus that approached. They started to stop them. So they weren't going to let us grab any buses. After a bit, my *compañero*, a guy who was in the committee and had stayed back around Huitzuco, he called my friend telling him that the *compas* had grabbed a bus out by Huitzuco, it was a Costa Line, but that when they got to the bus station they had been detained. They were being held there.

SANTIAGO FLORES, 24, FRESHMAN. We went to the Iguala tollbooth. We were hanging out with *Churro*, joking around. But at that time there were some police cars patrolling there, they were driving around and you know, I get a little scared just seeing them. What I did was look around to see where I'd run, thinking: "Okay, if they come after us, I'm going to run that way, head over that way, and grab rocks over there."

Behind us there was a fence and on the other side there was some construction, there were a bunch of rocks over there, like bricks that were already broken up. I thought: "Okay, there are rocks over there." But no, nothing happened. In fact, at the tollbooth, when the buses came up, they didn't pass through the tollbooth. They turned around and went back because the police were making the passengers get off and the bus didn't come through the tollbooth. We asked the passengers why the buses weren't driving through, and they told us because the bus had broken down. We were there for a while. After a time the committee told us to get back on the bus, that we were going to the bus station.

CARLOS MARTÍNEZ, 21, SOPHOMORE. After night fell a number of federal police squad cars started driving by. They went by and what they did was to stop the buses before the tollbooth and make everyone get off. The people came through the tollbooth on foot and the police sent the buses back. The police did that with at least three buses. And we asked the people that were walking through:

"Hey, why did they make you all get off the bus?"

"The feds told us to get off and walk."

We were on the Iguala side of the tollbooth and the feds were stopping the buses that were arriving in Iguala from Acapulco, from that direction, Tierra Colorada. The police stopped all the buses that came from that direction. The passengers all got out and walked, and the buses turned around and left. So we said:

"You know what? We need to go, because we're not going to be able to get anything here. We'll come back tomorrow, or we'll come up with something later."

We were making that decision to leave when a *compañero* who had stayed with the other bus out by Huitzuco called Bernardo and said:

"Hey, I'm here at the bus station, they've got me." We told him:

"Okay, wait there, we're gonna come get you right now." We all got back on the bus and we went to the bus station.

GERMÁN, 19, FRESHMAN. I lost track of my friends in the bus station. I didn't see them again. Once we got to the station we all spread out and I didn't know what happened to them. I got on the bus. We pulled in, I got off the bus, and then, all of a sudden, I turned around and got back on. The gunshots started around the plaza. And we shouted out to them to leave us alone, that we were on our way out of town. We kept driving through town and there were gunshots and gunshots and the *compas* who were running got back on the buses. They had been trying to talk with the police, so they would stop blocking us and let us go, because we really wanted to get back to the school, fear had taken hold of us by that point.

JOSÉ ARMANDO, 20, FRESHMAN. We grabbed another three buses and were on our way out. Some headed out toward the south, an Estrella de Oro bus and an Estrella Roja. We exited toward the north to get to the Periférico; the other three buses went that way. The first bus was a Costa Line, then another Costa Line, and the third bus was an Estrella de Oro. That's where we were. I was on the third bus when all of a sudden, as we were leaving the bus station in a caravan, the police pulled up and started shooting at us. We didn't have anything to protect ourselves with, because, you know, we're students. We got off the buses and wanted to defend ourselves with rocks to make the police get out of the way so we could keep going. I got off the bus. Most guys on the third bus didn't get off, they stayed on the bus because they were afraid. But a few of us got off, grabbed some rocks and threw them at the police trucks so they'd move out of the way and we could keep going.

IVÁN CISNEROS, 19, SOPHOMORE. We got to the bus station. They had the *compas* trapped there. We busted them out. Once we were in the station *Cochi* said that we needed to take some buses quickly. The drivers were there. We grabbed two Costa Line and an Estrella Roja. The Estrella Roja went one way out of the station and we went out another way, the way we had come in. We went straight through the center of Iguala, straight all the way to head out toward the state capital. The other *compas* had gone out the station exit. On the way, an Estrella de Oro bus went off another way. So we were just the two Costa Line buses and one Estrella de Oro.

ALEX ROJAS, FRESHMAN. The *compas* arrived. We talked to the guy in charge of the station. He said he didn't want any trouble, but the bus we were on was out of service. I think it needed some kind of liquid, I don't know, and that's why we couldn't take it. The *compañeros* said that was no problem, that they could get the liquid. Then we saw that the guy had started talking on the phone, and the bus station's security guards were on their radios. We figured they were letting someone know what was going on. What we did was leave as quickly as possible with the two Costa Line buses. I remember that the Estrella de Oro bus was parked out on the street, and we had the two Costa Line buses we meant to take back to the school with us. The *compañeros* started to get on the buses. I was going to get on the first Costa Line, but then I changed my mind.

I asked a *paisa* from the committee if we were only going to take those two buses or if we were going to grab another one. He told me we were going to take an Estrella Roja too. And so we did, we took the Estrella Roja. The two Costa Line buses went out first, a bit before, one or two minutes before, I think. Close enough that they went in a caravan with the Estrella de Oro bus. So those three buses left the station, but what I've heard is that the driver of the first bus took them deeper into Iguala. Instead of taking them out to the Periférico Sur, toward Chilpancingo, he took them deeper in toward the detour to Tierra Caliente, he was taking them in that direction. But we left the station in the Estrella Roja, going by the Aurrera[3] there in the city center, direct and fast to get to the Periférico Sur.

CARLOS MARTÍNEZ, 21, SOPHOMORE. Once we were there in the bus station a *compañero* told us to grab some buses.

"We should take the buses from here, let's grab them and go."

It was already night. We left in the buses. I got on the first one together with some others, maybe six or seven *compañeros* got on that bus. From the bus I could see that our *compañero* Bernardo was down there organizing, he was co-ordinating the activity. I wanted to get back off the bus and help him, but the freshman *compas* wouldn't let me. I said to them:

"Let me get by, I'm going to get off." Or: "Get out of the way."

But they didn't hear me and so I stayed on the bus. And that bus was the first to leave the station, it went in the lead, the first bus that you see in all the photos. I was there with other *compañeros*. I didn't see Bernardo again. The image I have of him is being down there directing everything.

COYUCO BARRIENTOS, 21, FRESHMAN. We got to the bus station and started to spread out. Some *compañeros* went into the station. We started to take some buses. We grabbed three in total. And we had two other buses that we brought from the school. There were five. We started to leave. The first two buses went ahead. I was in the third bus of the five. We were in the middle of the caravan, but

___
3. A Mexican supermarket chain.

the other two buses took a different route and we didn't see where they had gone. So we arrived at the point where there is a *zócalo*. And the driver was going really slowly. He wasn't getting very far. And I think that he gave the authorities time to arrive and try to get us off the buses. The driver was moving at a snail's pace. I was in the middle of the bus and I shouted out to the *compañeros* up front to make the driver step on it, and if not they should get him out of the way and drive the bus themselves, that we had to hurry up. If we didn't, we'd get caught there. And the driver went even more slowly; he didn't pay any attention to us. In part, I blame the bus driver because he gave them time to arrive. It's just that, that night, we didn't know, no one knew there was a government event, that the director of the DIF[4] was giving a speech right there in the *zócalo*. In fact, a number of newspapers say that we went to protest her speech. But that isn't true. We were only going to our action, which was asking for donations and grabbing buses, and that was it. We didn't even know about the government event.

SANTIAGO FLORES, 24, FRESHMAN. We got on the bus and took off. The driver didn't want to go because he said he was sick, or something like that, that he had to get some medicine, or go to the doctor, he was saying something like that. He didn't want to go, he refused, and a *compa* from the committee took the keys from him and said that he'd drive.

The driver said no, because if he left the bus the company would hold him responsible, I think. So he said that he would drive.

When we were leaving the station the driver said

---

4. The Sistema Nacional para el Desarrollo Integral de la Familia (DIF) is a federal social services program.

something strange, that he didn't know the way. That was strange, that he would say he didn't know how to get out of town. The *compas* were saying if he worked for the bus company he had to know how to get to the bus station, but he said he didn't, that he didn't know how to get out of town, he didn't know the streets there. We left, but really slowly, the driver was going slowly. Around then, there's a . . . what's it called? I think in the center there is some kind of plaza, I think, a *zócalo*. I was in a window seat and I saw people having dinner. We went a few meters farther and I heard something like firecrackers. I thought they were fireworks, but the *compas* said: "They're shooting at us."

JUAN PÉREZ, 25, FRESHMAN. We went to the bus station. Everyone got on a bus and we left. In some buses twenty students got on, in others fifteen, in others ten, and so on. We left the station and we realized there were police trucks following us. A few blocks later a police truck pulled in front of the lead bus. A police officer got out of the truck and started running, shooting in the air. I was in the lead bus. All of us *compañeros* got off the bus to push the squad truck out of the way. Once we started pushing it, the driver backed up and took off. We kept going down the street. We were lost and so started asking people for directions.

"Hey, you, excuse me, sir: Is this the way to Chilpo?"

"Yeah, keep going straight."

COYUCO BARRIENTOS, 21, FRESHMAN. And so a municipal police squad truck pulled up and cut us off just at the *zócalo*. The police officers in the back all got out and only the driver stayed inside. So the *compañeros* in the front of the lead bus threw rocks at the squad truck to make it move. They did that because the police started shooting. At first they shot in the air, but then they started shooting at us. That's why the *compañeros* took action. They threw rocks at the truck, smashing its windshield. The other cops ran. And more police were running toward the *zócalo*, shooting behind them, not even looking to see if they were. . . . I mean, not looking to see if they could hurt someone who wasn't even involved. But the police driver moved the squad truck and we kept going. The *compañeros* that had gotten off the bus stayed in the street, running next to the bus to repel another attack. We kept going forward.

CARLOS MARTÍNEZ, 21, SOPHOMORE. The guy driving the bus told us that he didn't know his way around Iguala, that the bus was broken down, that he had a commitment at a certain time with his wife, you know, an endless list of excuses so that he drove really slowly. He was driving so slowly on purpose, as if he knew something. Who knows? But he drove the bus really slowly.

At that point, a police truck pulled in front of us. I saw through the bus window when the squad truck pulled in front and a number of police got out of the back aiming at us. The *compañeros* got off the bus. The police started to shoot in the air. We started to hear gunshots—a lot of gunshots. That was where the first shootings began. I got off the bus and when the police began to shoot I threw myself to the ground. The bullets were breaking glass. You could hear the glass breaking, and pieces of it started to fall on my back.

A few blocks later I started to hear music. I looked around and realized that we were at the Iguala *zócalo*, but people were running and soon the music shut off and everyone started running. By this time all the *compañeros* who had gotten off the bus, we were all running, fleeing while being shot at. We passed the *zócalo*. I remember I was running with a number of freshman *compañeros*. I crossed the *zócalo* and what we did was get back on the first bus. The bus had kept going, slowly, so we caught up with it and got back on, the first one like before. The bus kept going.

MIGUEL ALCOCER, 20, FRESHMAN. The police started shooting. The *compañeros* said that the police were shooting in the air, and I think they were. So many squad trucks started arriving. There were three buses in a caravan and I was in the lead bus. I don't know much about Iguala, but we were on a straight street and on that street the municipal police would pull out from the intersections. At that time the shots were coming directly at us. The driver kept going straight ahead and the police would drive up and shoot at us. Some *compañeros* under the stress of being shot at got off the bus and picked up rocks. I think there is a *zócalo* around there. I don't know what was going on, but there was some kind of a park and there were a lot of people around. A municipal police officer cut us off around there. The squad truck blocked us and the cops shot directly at us. There were also police shooting at us from behind. You couldn't run anywhere. So some *compañeros* managed to find some rocks and threw them at the squad truck and broke the windshield. So the cop moved the truck out of the way and we were able to keep going.

EDGAR YAIR, 18, FRESHMAN. At first the police were shooting in the air. We weren't scared because never. . . . Well, we knew that they couldn't shoot at us because we're students and they can't do that to people like us. We kept going and at every street corner we passed, police squad trucks pulled out, and the bullets were coming more and more directly at us each time. And we had rocks. . . . Whatever we could find. We threw the rocks at the police because they were shooting at us. There were three buses in a caravan. I was in the second bus. We drove down that whole avenue and the cops didn't even care that there were so many other people around, kids, women, all kinds of people. And the cops didn't respect those people. As we drove along the avenue, we didn't care about anything, what we cared about was getting out of there as soon as possible.

IVÁN CISNEROS, 19, SOPHOMORE. We came to what I think was the *zócalo*, or something like that, I couldn't see well, when the first municipal police trucks started pulling up. They didn't tell us to stop; they just pulled out in front and starting cocking their guns and aiming at us. And that's when we got angry, because before, when we were asking for donations on the highway, the federal police would show up with the same attitude, cocking their weapons, but we would instantly tell them that we were students, and unarmed. And then the police would think about it and their commander or the person in charge would tell them to lower their guns. And so that's what we did, it's kind of like a truce, when we say: "We're students, we don't have any weapons," and we show our empty hands in the air, that we're unarmed, that was when, before, the police would lower their weapons and we'd have to start some kind of dialogue. That's the way it had been before.

For example, the state police in Chilpancingo say to us: "Young men, you can't grab vehicles like that, you have to come to an agreement with the bus companies and blah, blah, blah," stuff like that. But at that moment, the police didn't act like that. We said:

"We're students, we're unarmed," but the police didn't give a shit. They kept aiming at us and that's when we heard the first gunshots from the back of the caravan. I told the others to get off the bus and grab rocks. We started pelting the squad truck that was blocking us. That truck took off, but we still heard gunshots coming from behind. They kept shooting, but I think they were shooting in the air. At that moment, we ran ahead to stop traffic from the side streets so that the bus could get through. All along the way we kept hearing gunshots, they popped in the air.

ERNESTO GUERRERO, 23, FRESHMAN. Leaving the bus station we made it about a block and a half when the first two police squad trucks came out of nowhere. At no point did they signal for us to stop, at no point did they try to speak with us, they simply started firing their weapons in the air. We were in a caravan of three buses: the two Costa Line buses that we had just taken, and an Estrella de Oro that was in the rear. I was in that bus, the third one. When we heard the gunshots, one of the sophomore *compas* who was with us said:

"Don't be scared, *paisas*, they're shooting in the air."

But when we got off the bus we saw that they were not just shooting in the air, but also shooting at the bus, and they started aiming at us. That's when we made the decision to defend ourselves. How? In the road there I found four rocks, and four rocks are what I threw. We didn't have any choice. We had to defend ourselves with whatever was around, or let them kill us without putting up any defense.

At least I'm of the opinion that if they're going to kill me, at least let it be while I'm defending myself. And, well, I found four rocks and I threw four rocks. It was obvious that the municipal police wanted to take our lives. The gunshots were aimed at the bus and at those of us who had gotten off the bus. That was when we decided to get back on the buses. We ran a bit farther down the road. The Iguala police were still shooting at the buses. I didn't find any more rocks.

How was I to defend myself? I ran. The third bus in the caravan closed its door. The second bus had its door closed too. I ran up to the first bus and that was when I was able to jump on. I stayed there in the entrance, by the door of the first bus.

ANDRÉS HERNÁNDEZ, 21, FRESHMAN. The police had already blown out the tires of the first bus, where I was riding. I realized this when a squad truck pulled out in front of us and parked there to block our way. All the police got out of the squad truck, hid around the street corners and shot at us. So what we did was run up to the squad truck to push it out of the way. We were pushing the truck when a second squad truck came within six or seven meters of us. It pulled up and the police shot at us, brutally, without thinking twice about it. They shot at us and that was when the first *compañero*, a student in my group named Aldo Gutiérrez Solano, fell. When we saw that he had fallen it enraged us. We wanted to escape, but the police were shooting at us, so we ran back to hide behind the first bus. In my case, I was there behind the first bus, taking shelter.

CARLOS MARTÍNEZ, 21, SOPHOMORE. We were driving along Álvarez Avenue. Through the window I could see the Periférico. We were so close to turning onto the Periférico when a police truck pulled in front of us. It was a municipal police Ranger-type truck. But something strange happened there. The squad truck pulled up with a guy driving it, and that guy got out, fled, and left the truck there, in contrast to the first time a police truck pulled in front of us and the cop driving then moved it out of the way. This time the cop left the truck there in the middle of the road. And so we got off the bus. I, Aldo, Malboro, a number of us got off the bus and tried to move the police truck. Imagine that this is the truck, here is the hood, and here is the back of the truck. I was here at the back trying to move the truck and Aldo was in front of me. We tried to move the truck out of the way. And then I heard when the shots began, loud. I ducked like this and when I looked at the ground that was when Aldo fell with a shot to the head and there was so much blood coming from the wound, too much blood, too much. I went into shock looking at his body for about three seconds; the shots were still ringing out and I just stood there, looking. Luckily, I wasn't hit.

"Run," we shouted, "run!"

We went to the space between the first and second buses. We stayed there throughout the shooting. Only those of us who were riding on the first and second buses took shelter there. We were about twenty *compañeros* between the two buses and there were police in front of us and police behind us shutting off any escape. They shot at us like you wouldn't believe, there were so many gunshots, it was intense. At first I couldn't imagine that they were shooting at us, I couldn't even imagine that they would kill us. I thought the sounds were, who knows, bottle rockets or some kind of firecracker like that. But when I started seeing the bullets, the bullet shells, I realized they were going to kill us, I realized that they wanted to kill every single one of us.

Aldo was lying in the street for a long time. We started to call ambulances. We called 066 so they'd send ambulances. The number 066 is a federal number. It's impossible for the federal government to say that they didn't know what was happening, that the federal police didn't know, because 066 channels information to the local branch of the federal police that is next to an army base.

SANTIAGO FLORES, 24, FRESHMAN. Farther down the road the police started coming out from the street corners. They started shooting at us again, and when we came up to a mini-Aurrera that was where a police truck shut us off. We got off the buses. We threw rocks at them, but the police got out of the truck and left it there in the middle of the street. We couldn't keep driving, we were stuck. Other students told us to move the truck. I got off the bus, others got off the bus too. I don't know if it was from fear or desperation, but we couldn't move the truck. I remember that Aldo, the student who is brain dead, was there with us. I was in the front, at one of the headlights, pushing toward the back. There were about four of us there. Others were in back of the truck pushing it forward. I mean, I don't know if it was because we were so scared or desperate, but some *compas* were pushing from behind and we were pushing from the front and none of us had a clue: they were pushing this way and we were pushing that way. We didn't coordinate, you know, we didn't know what to do. And another student was in the driver's seat steering the wheel this way and that, but no way, we couldn't move it. And that was when they started shooting at us, firing at us. More police trucks were arriving. And so what I did was put my hands behind my head like this, duck down and run. I wanted to throw myself to the ground because of all the shooting. You could hear the bullets whizzing by.

When we were getting to the space between the first and second buses I heard that the *compas* were shouting that one of us had been shot. "You shot one of us!" But the police didn't pay any attention to them. They kept shooting and shooting. "You killed another one of us, you killed another, stop shooting!" But the police didn't care. We raised our hands in the air to show that we weren't going to do anything to them, that we surrendered, but the cops didn't care. We asked them for help, saying: "Help us, he's still alive!" Because a couple of *compas* said that they saw that Aldo was raising his hand, they said he was still alive. They screamed: "Help us, don't be assholes, he's still alive!" But the cops ignored them.

The shooting lasted a long time, so, so, so much time before they brought an ambulance. The ambulance took some twenty or twenty-five minutes to arrive. It took so long to arrive, but that was when they took the *compa*. We were there, shouting that we would turn ourselves in and the police ignored us. You looked around the edge of the bus and they shot at you. You held out your hand and they shot at you. One *compa* who stepped out from the buses, a bullet cut right here across his chest, the bullet sliced right across.

JORGE, 20, FRESHMAN. They were shooting at us all down the street, they were chasing us up to this intersection, I don't know what it's called. That's where the police truck cut us off. The police got out and left the truck there. Since we wanted to keep going, with a number of *compañeros*, we got off the bus to move the truck. When we were moving the truck, the police ran back to take cover and from there they began to shoot at us. We were trying to quickly move the truck when they started shooting at us. And almost immediately a *compañero* fell when they shot him in the head. Well, I got scared and, you know, seeing how he fell, the majority of us ran and hid behind the first bus. Some of us jumped quickly aboard the first bus. From there we could see that the *compañero* who got shot was still alive, he was still moving. The bus driver told us to go get him out of the street but when we tried to get off the bus again, the police shot at us. We couldn't get back off the bus. There were about ten of us who got back on the bus. So we went to the back of the bus and took cover there while the police were shooting at us. They didn't stop shooting. We shouted out to them, but they ignored us.

IVÁN CISNEROS, 19, SOPHOMORE. We were coming to the intersection of Juan N. Álvarez and Periférico to head out toward Chilpo when police truck 002 came out of nowhere and cut us off. We got off the bus and went to move the truck. The police officers all got out of the truck and ran. When we tried to move the truck we heard the police shooting at us. That was when they hit Aldo, who was beside me. I ducked down and grabbed the truck to push it from the bottom and start to move it, lift it, push it and that was when they hit the *compañero* Aldo. He went down. When we saw that he fell we all froze, as they say, and we got scared for real then. We saw that this had gotten real serious. When we had heard the gunshots we said, "Those are shots in the air," but who knew?

When we saw that the *compañero* went down, that was when the fear hit. We started to shout to the *compañeros* on the bus: "*Compas*, get down here!" We screamed to the police that they had killed a *compañero*, because we thought that the guy was dead. With a bullet to the head, you'd think that someone would die instantly. But he was just bleeding. We ran to the back of the first bus. We tried to take Aldo with us, but the bullets were flying by so close, we couldn't do anything. We left the *compañero* there and went to the space behind the bus. We shouted to the *compañeros* on the second bus to come down, and we wanted to shout the same to those on the third bus, but the police were already machine-gunning that bus. We couldn't see it, we just heard the shots. We shouted out to the police that they had already killed one of us, that what more did they want, that they had already fulfilled their mission. We shouted out to them, sarcastically: "You should act so tough with the *narcos*!" We didn't know that they were also the *narcos*. We tried to help the *compañeros* on the third bus, but as soon as we peeked around the edge of the bus, as soon as we tried to do anything, the police fired at us and the bullets flew over the concrete. We couldn't leave from behind that part of the bus, between the first and second buses.

When they shot the *compañero*, we started making calls to the students back here on campus. We called David, the student president. We called the other *compañeros* to tell them we were being shot at. I started to post about it on the social networks, that we were being shot at, that people should call the press or any media, that we were in Iguala, and they had killed one *compañero*. I started to post photos of the *compañero* who had been shot. I called my dad and told him what was happening. He told me to stay calm, and that the most that they could do was arrest us and beat the crap out of everyone. He thought that they would have to eventually let us all go.

At that point I was thinking: "Okay, well, fuck it, they're going to grab us." When we saw that more squad trucks were arriving, we thought: "They're going to corral us, they're going to come at us from both sides, and they're going to arrest us." But that's what we were thinking, you know, that they were just going to arrest us. This is what we thought: "Yes, they're going to beat the shit out of us, but we'll be okay when it's all over."

JUAN PÉREZ, 25, FRESHMAN. Once we could see the highway just up ahead, a police truck shut us off; it pulled in front of us, the driver jumped out and ran, leaving the squad truck there in the road. The bus stopped. The bus following us also stopped. A bunch of us *compañeros* got off the first bus and tried to move the truck out of the way. About fifteen *compañeros* were at the front of the truck to push it. My *compañero*—we called him *Garra*, The Claw—and I were in the back of the truck. There were just two of us there. In a matter of seconds the cops shot at us, and in that instant a bullet hit his head. He went down, falling slowly. We screamed:

"A *compañero* is down!"

In that moment all of the *compañeros* that were at the front of the truck ran; they all ran. I was about two meters from the bus. There were about ten of us that ran to the bus and I was able to jump inside the door at the very end, landing on top of the other *compañeros*. I don't even know where the cop came from, but he shot me in my left knee. I don't know if it hurt or didn't hurt. I just jumped inside the bus. Then, I went to the first seat and lay down and said to a *compañero*:

"I think they got me."

"Really?"

"Yeah, they got me," I said and grabbed my leg and just saw blood. I dragged myself toward the back of the bus, to the last seat at the back. *Compañeros* asked me:

"*Camarada*, are you okay?"

"I'm okay," I said, "don't worry about me, but if the police come inside the bus we can't give up, if they take anyone, they'll have to take us all."

JOSÉ ARMANDO, 20, FRESHMAN. About five of us went out to put a T-shirt under the *compañero* Aldo's head because he was still moving, we could see him move and we went to put something under his head because he had already lost so much blood. That was when they shot at us more intensely, and we took cover behind the squad truck. Aldo had fallen behind the truck. We took cover behind the wheel, all of us pressed together, and then we ran back to the space behind the first bus. The police had been coming closer to us. They were coming to take us away. Everyone was erasing all their contacts form their cell phones because we thought they were coming to take us—like they always do when they repress us—off to jail or the police station where they go through our cell phones. So, that's why we were erasing all our contacts. That's what we thought would happen. That or that they'd kill us all right there.

During the time we were in between the two buses another *compañero* started dying. He fell to the ground because he already had some kind of a lung illness. He fell, he was having trouble breathing, and we shouted out to the police for them to call an ambulance, but no. So we called the ambulance and we explained to them where we were and why we needed an ambulance. We told them that we were being shot at, that they should send the ambulance as fast as possible because otherwise the *compañero* would die, and that they needed to take Aldo as well.

EDGAR YAIR, 18, FRESHMAN. Like I told you, we had thought that they wouldn't shoot directly at us. I mean, we thought they were shooting at the ground or something like that. But then we saw the *compañero* hit with a bullet to the head, and he fell to the ground. There were about eight of us trying to move the truck. Only three of us realized that the *compañero* had been shot in the head. The other *compañeros* didn't realize what had just happened. With all the adrenaline they didn't realize, until we screamed to them to stop pushing the truck, because it was almost right on top of the *compañero*. We screamed loudly for them to stop, that a *compañero* had been wounded, but they couldn't hear us because of the noise of the gunshots and all the yelling. They didn't understand what we were saying. Finally we gestured to them and they realized that the *compañero* was on the ground, bleeding from a gunshot to the head. We wanted to lift him up, but instead of letting us, the police shot at us more intensely, firing rapid bursts of shots.

We ran to a place between the two buses. A number of *compañeros* took shelter there, we were maybe twenty-seven there, I think. And we were there for a long time, almost two hours. We screamed to the police that we were unarmed, that we had nothing to hurt them with. We screamed for them to stop shooting at us, because if you leaned out just a bit, they shot at you. They didn't feel the slightest pity seeing us all sad and afraid. We were all really nervous, really scared by everything that was happening, seeing how our *compañero* was still lying out in the street, convulsing. We wanted to go get him, but the police wouldn't let us, they shot at us. At last an ambulance arrived.

MIGUEL ALCOCER, 20, FRESHMAN. They got off the bus to move the truck out of the way so we could get out of there fast, leave Iguala. That was when we heard the first shots and Aldo went down. Now they were shooting to kill us. They were no longer shooting in the air, but at us. The *compañeros* hid between the first and second buses. A number of us were still in the first bus, standing. I and ten or so other *compañeros* were about to get off the bus when a cop saw us and shot straight at us. He stood right out in front, like this, and opened fire. I threw myself back inside the bus. One *compañero* got hit in the leg and screamed. I thought they had killed him, that he had been hit, screamed, and had fallen. All my *compañeros* said that he had been killed but no, in that same instant he called out for help. We helped him get to the back of the bus and wrap his leg. And we stayed there.

We spoke out to our friends down between the two buses that we were inside the first bus. The *compañeros* were also taking shelter there because if the police saw you so much as peek out they shot at you. The police wouldn't let you even look around the corner of the bus. The police had posted themselves at opposite street corners and from there were shooting and shooting at my *compañeros*. And we were stuck inside the bus. We thought that they'd come for us and they'd take us to jail. We already assumed that we'd just be taken to jail. And there we were all lying on the floor. Some *compañeros* were crying because we were being shot at.

Then I heard that my *compañeros* in the back were shouting out to the police that we were students from the teachers college and that we were unarmed. And the police shouted back that they didn't give a fuck. They said:

"You are all about to be fucked."

And, well, I think that my *compañeros*, the ones who were crying, felt even more helpless hearing the police say that. And, in all honesty, we were really scared because they were shooting straight at us. And the *compañeros* shouted out for the police to call an ambulance for the *compa* who was wounded. One cop told us that we had no idea where we were. He said:

"Sure, maybe they'll find your *compañero*, but dead, or maybe they'll never find him." He said that to us.

All my *compañeros* screamed at the police to calm down. And still the police shouted to us:

"Throw out your weapons!"

And we were like, what weapons are we going to throw out if we don't have any? As one *compañero* said:

"This is absurd, we should have been armed so that at least one of them would have been cut down, and we wouldn't have been the only ones dying."

ERNESTO GUERRERO, 23, FRESHMAN. As we arrived at the Iguala Periférico a squad truck cut us off. We couldn't get around it, and a bunch of municipal police trucks were following us. They corralled us, they shut us in. Immediately, a number of *compañeros* on the first bus, we decided to get off the bus and push the squad truck. When we got off the bus the first *compañero* to get to the truck was Aldo. I came up behind him. We started pushing the truck and the gunshots started. Immediately they hit Aldo in the head. I turned and saw him. A pool of blood formed and I screamed to my *compañeros*: "They hit one of us!" Another *compañero* came up and we tried to pull Aldo behind the truck, but the police machine-gunned us. We couldn't help him. At first we thought he was dead. A group of about twenty of us took cover between the first and second buses. The others weren't able to get off the first bus and stayed in there. They ducked down so as not to be seen by the police. We had nowhere to go. They were shooting at us from the front and from behind. Those of us who had gotten off the bus took cover between the two buses. The *compañeros* on the third bus, the Estrella de Oro, were surrounded. The police held them all at gunpoint and started to make them get off the bus and lie facedown on the street with their hands behind their heads.

After a while a Red Cross ambulance came for Aldo. We saw that he had been moving and called the ambulance. It came, took Aldo, and the police kept aiming their guns at us. If you moved, they shot at you. If you spoke, they shot at you. In other words, you couldn't do anything without them shooting at you. The municipal police were firing whole clips at us. And then after shooting they'd take the time to pick up the shells. I shouted:

"Why are you picking up the bullet shells?" Well, because they knew the bullshit they were doing. And they mocked us, they laughed, they aimed at my *compañeros* being arrested and at us.

And then a *compañero* who suffers from a lung condition had a crisis. He had had a lung operation before and he was dying on us there. His eyes were more gone than here. He was fading and we called another ambulance. The operators came out with the ridiculous story that they didn't know where we were.

"I don't know where that place is," they told us, "we went and didn't see you all, we couldn't find the address." That ambulance never arrived. Squad truck 302 arrived.

EDGAR YAIR, 18, FRESHMAN. When we were all bunched together between the two buses, a *compañero* suffering from a lung problem had some kind of crisis with his lungs, and so he fainted. It was like he was having a heart attack, or who knows. We carried him and laid him down on the ground so that the police could pick him up. And the police, instead of picking him up carefully because he was sick, grabbed him like a dog, dragged him, and threw him in the back of a squad truck and drove off with him.

COYUCO BARRIENTOS, 21, FRESHMAN. I was going to get off of the bus when I looked toward where a *compañero* was lying in a pool of blood, convulsing. A *compañero* next to him tried to help him when a bullet whizzed right by. The other *compañeros* were still trying to move the truck out of the way so that we could keep going. They didn't see that the *compañero* had fallen almost under the truck. They almost pushed the truck over him. The others shouted out to them to stop, that there was a *compañero* down on the ground. They were able to stop them from pushing the truck, but what they couldn't do was move the *compañero* who had been shot, because the police were still firing on them. The police didn't stop firing. Those *compañeros* had to leave the wounded student there and run to take cover behind the bus. And the police started shooting straight at us then. There were a number of bullet holes in the windshield. Another *compañero* and I were about to get off, standing on the edge of the stairs when the police started to shoot at us there in the doorway. If I hadn't pulled him toward me he would have been hit too. I pulled him and we both fell to the floor. I shouted to the others still on the bus not to try to get off, but to run towards the back of the bus. Everyone was all tangled up. As best I could, I started jumping toward the back, jumping over the seats and hearing bullets pass by my body. Luckily none of them hit me.

I fell between the seats, and the others who were up front leapt and stepped over me. It was like that, one jumping over another, the other stepping on someone else, all of us rushing to the back of the bus. And in those circumstances, it makes sense. We were really afraid, and you try to escape as best you can. We were all taking cover. One *compañero* told us that a bullet had grazed his leg. We asked those close to him to check him out. But he said that he was okay, that the bullet had only grazed him, that he was fine, that it wasn't a big deal.

The police kept shooting at us. The only thing I thought to do was call the *compañeros* back at the college, those on the committee. I have their cell numbers. I called:

"*Compa*, we are getting fucked, the police are kicking the shit out of us. They are shooting at anything that moves! They already killed . . . they hit one *compa*. He's convulsing and bleeding to death. Get over here! We need help!" The *compañero* didn't understand. Like he was in shock. He didn't react.

"Fuck man," I said, "This is Coyuco, I'm Coyuco the freshman. You've all got to come, the police are attacking us, we don't have any rocks. They've got us corralled near an Aurrera. Get here as fast as you can! Somebody's wounded. Who knows how many more wounded there are behind us. They stopped some other *compañeros* and they're taking them into some kind of building. The police won't stop shooting."

I couldn't see well where we were. I didn't know the name of the street yet. And you could still hear the gunshots from the police. Some police left, and others arrived. After a bit I saw an ambulance come, but the police sent it back. After that, a bit later, it came back again and that was when, I think, that they took the *compañero* who was wounded.

There was another *compañero* who had had a lung operation about a month earlier, I think. And he, maybe from all the adrenaline, I don't know, or all the fear, the fright, he was also convulsing. He had a panic attack. They told the police that another *compañero* was hurt, that they shouldn't be, you know, assholes, and that they should help us. And, well, the police stopped shooting, they relaxed a bit, so the *compas* could show them the wounded *compañero* who needed help. And what we saw was how the fucking cops grabbed him like an animal. They dragged him along by one hand and one foot. When they put him in the back of the squad truck, they tossed him like an animal, like he was some sack of flour. They took him away. The *compañeros* were able to see that it was squad truck number 302.

ERICK SANTIAGO LÓPEZ, 22, SOPHOMORE. I was riding in the third bus, the Estrella de Oro. The police were shooting at us. I got off three times with a fire extinguisher to throw at them. At that point they didn't shoot me. I was incredibly lucky. And that was when we saw police with different uniforms. Because in all the testimonies it just says that the municipal police participated. They never talked about the federal police and the state police. I was standing up in the front of the bus, next to the driver. The driver, who is taller than me, was the one who shook up the fire extinguisher and gave it to me. He shook it up and said:

"Dude, throw this at them. It will explode, and then you all can get out of here, and that way I'll be able to get out of here too."

I was able to throw it at the police, but in the instant that I threw the extinguisher, that was when they shot me. I stood next to the driver, in the door. I was able to stick my hand out, like this. Just when I threw the extinguisher like this, that's when I took the bullet. I threw the extinguisher at the police and in the same instant the police shot me in my right arm. They shot me and that was when we realized we were done.

Since I was one of the organizers that night and was riding with the *compañero Cochiloco*, that's when I said: "You know what, call the secretary." At that time the secretary was *La Parca*, The Reaper. We called *La Parca*. We waited about ten minutes on board the bus, then *Cochiloco* told the driver:

"Open the door, we're going to give ourselves up. We can't keep fighting, they've already shot my friend."

The *compas* were terrified. They didn't know what to do. My arm was hurting me. All the tendons were destroyed. The five tendons connecting my fingers were destroyed. All this part of my skin was destroyed. When we got off the bus the police stood to the side of the door and started to pull us out and to put our hands behind our heads. Since the driver was the first one off, they pulled him aside, off to a corner away from the rest of us. I'd been shot, but they treated me just like all the others; they put my hands behind my head. And they started to throw us down on the ground.

"Shut up, you son of a bitch," they said, "you are beyond fucked." And after a bit they said: "If you are all such bad-asses, then let's see it now, fucking *ayotzinapos*." Just imagine, there they were with their guns and all of us with nothing at all. That's when one loses hope, because they are all armed and if you move they shoot you. We stayed like that. I remember all my *compañeros* were down on the ground. My *compañero Cochiloco* tried to stand up to them and they beat him. He was tough, in that he wasn't going to just surrender. So they grabbed him and beat him in the stomach with the butt of a rifle. When they knocked him to the ground, then they started beating him in the face.

"Kill the one you shot in the arm," one cop said to another, "put a bullet in him." The cop came up to me and stuck his weapon, an AR-15, right to my head. He put the gun against my head, and maybe he thought about it and said: "And if I kill him?"

I thought to myself: "Well, I guess this is it." And then, just seconds later, he moved his rifle away from my forehead, right here next to my temple, and then he himself called an ambulance. When he called the ambulance I was aware of everything that was going on. The guy who was next to me had wrapped a bandanna around my arm when we were still on the bus. We called him *Botas*, Boots. When I was thrown on the ground, that guy was crying. He saw it when they put the gun to my head. He saw it when they hit me in the ribs because I had tried to lift myself up. He knew that if I tried to act tough, the cop would kill me. During this time I saw a federal police uniform, on the back it said FEDERAL POLICE. And there was a state police officer next to him.

When they tried to make me lie back down, I just lay on my side. I was looking out toward the Periférico. Two civilians arrived and got out of their car. I don't know if they were the leaders. They weren't wearing masks. One of them had a pistol. They were giving orders and the others were obeying them.

The cops grabbed me and put me in an ambulance. They went through all my things. They took a small black cell phone that I had with me. And when they put me in the ambulance, that was when they started to put my *compañeros* in the different squad trucks. I could see it. None of the kids said a word. They were crying. I couldn't see all the others, but they were all lying in the street. Not one of them spoke. Not one of them said: "Why are you doing this to us?"

If they hadn't shot me I would also be disappeared. The bullet saved me. Everyone who was riding in the bus where I was is now disappeared. I was the only one who was saved. All the blood that was in the bus. . . . In fact, I have some photos here. This is the photo of my arm where they shot me. All that blood is mine.

JORGE HERNÁNDEZ ESPINOSA, 20, FRESHMAN. I had gone with a *compañero* to play a volleyball game in Tixtla. We went to play at six in the afternoon, when they had all gone to Iguala. We played the game and went back to the school around ten o'clock. On our way to dinner we saw people running in all directions, even the seniors. We didn't pay any attention to them. Then a *paisa* from the committee told us:

"Everyone to the parking lot."

It was around ten-thirty when we went to the parking lot, and that was when we found out. But they only told us:

"There are problems in Iguala." And we thought that it was the same as always: "So, they're not letting our *compañeros* leave." Then they called us to go to the outdoor basketball court [which has a corrugated tin roof, but no walls]. We went there and it was there that they told us that a freshman had been shot in the head. They didn't know if he was dead or alive. An ambulance had taken him off, and that was all that they told us. Then they started to look for buses, but couldn't find the drivers, or the buses didn't have any gas. They said: "Some of you freshmen get in the Urvan."[5] Several juniors and seniors as well as some freshmen got in, including me. I was in the first Urvan that got to Iguala.

OMAR GARCÍA, 24, SOPHOMORE. They called the school and we learned what was going on. We called the media, the radio stations, the teachers union, and the people who support us. We were in a state of absolute alarm, trying to figure out what we could do. It all happened very fast. We organized about thirty people and—well, we took off. When we got there, there *were* federal police in the streets, in the area near the army base. We came into town right around there. There were federal police patrolling, and the state police were posted at the entrance to the city. There was a state police roadblock on the way into town. But they didn't stop us.

EDGAR ANDRÉS VARGAS, 20, JUNIOR. Since I was already in my third year, I didn't really follow the activities that the freshmen and the committee organized. But that day I was washing clothes outside and the guy they call *Cochiloco*, who is disappeared, was there with another kid and they were shouting out to a guy whose room was right by there. They were shouting for him to join them on an action, that they were going to hijack some buses for the march. He didn't say where. The kid who was in his room on the second floor, who was also in the Struggle Committee, was

_____
5. A Nissan van common in Mexico.

saying he wouldn't go because it was *Cochiloco*'s turn. And that was how I heard about the action. But you know, it was just another action. I kept washing, hung my clothes out to dry, and that was that. I went back to my room. I remember that I called my parents because we had our classroom observations coming up, and I called my parents to ask them for some money. They said yes and asked me to wait a few days and then they'd send it. I lay down on my bed, took out a folder I needed for some homework, but didn't have the photocopies I needed, so I left it for the following day. And so I lay down, turned on the computer and logged in to Facebook. Just then a friend called me. As we were talking, a kid came in screaming for everyone to get ready because there were problems, the freshmen were under attack.

We all ran outside immediately. I told my friend that I'd call her back. She asked me what was going on and I told her nothing, and then just hung up. I put on my pants, my tennis shoes. I wasn't wearing a T-shirt, but grabbed my red Ayotzi jacket and put that on without a shirt underneath. We went to the basketball court and they were saying that the freshmen were trapped and we needed to go help them. Several of my friends were there and they were going, so I went as well. I ran back to my room for a T-shirt, the first one I saw, and then ran back with the white T-shirt in my hand. I think the committee secretaries were in Chilpo and we didn't have any more buses, or there were buses, but the drivers weren't there. So we got an Urvan, we all got in, a bunch of us from my study group. Everything happened so fast. We took off for Iguala. One *compa* had told me not to go, because I had mentioned to him earlier that my girlfriend would be coming to visit me. I think she was going to arrive around dawn. I didn't think anything so serious was happening, since there've always been problems, and when

I go they've never been so serious, so I got on the Urvan and left. There were some freshmen and sophomores with us. The Urvan was so full that it couldn't go very fast even though the driver was flooring it.

Since Iguala is a bit far—I don't know exactly, but maybe two hours—while we were on the road all the kids were calling their *compañeros* in Iguala. A number of them didn't answer, their phones rang but no one picked up. A bunch of the kids on the Urvan were making calls and no one answered. Later, when we were coming into Iguala, at the entrance to town, beneath a bridge, I think, we saw an Estrella de Oro bus. We thought that it was the students, at that moment we thought it was their bus.

All the bus's windows were busted, and the bus was all shot up. But that bus was on the other side of the highway, and when we came into Iguala there were a lot of police trucks patrolling. We passed that bus and then one of the guys in the Urvan shouted for us to stop because he had seen some students. I don't know if they were there, actually, I didn't see them out there on the highway. But this other guy had seen five or six. But the Urvan couldn't turn around there, we had to go up to a place where we could turn around and come back. But we went back and didn't see anyone. We went back two times and didn't see them. Then we pulled into an OXXO convenience store and someone called, I don't know who, to let them know where we were. The guy who was driving is in my class and he wasn't familiar with Iguala. He got out and asked a taxi driver:

"How do I get to such-and-such place?"

The taxi driver told him more or less how to get there and we drove off. I think we got to the center of Iguala. There was a little park, I don't know what it was, a small plaza. We stopped again. There were police trucks everywhere.

When we saw a police truck approaching we all ducked down so they wouldn't see us. We were scared they'd arrest us too. They were municipal police. There was one small police car, but I couldn't see what it was. The majority were municipal police, and one state police truck. I saw a state police truck when we were in the park. It passed right by us in the street. I don't know how the other Urvan got there, but I heard that they were in Chilpancingo and went from there to Iguala. There in the center some people told us how to get to the place where the students were. And then we got there.

SERGIO OCAMPO, 58, JOURNALIST WITH THE AUTONOMOUS UNIVERSITY OF GUERRERO RADIO STATION AND CHILPANCINGO-BASED STAFF WRITER FOR *LA JORNADA*. I was about to have dinner when someone close to the mayor called me and said that there were shootings in Iguala.

"Hey, they are shooting at the students," some journalist friends then told me. I didn't believe it, really. At that time it was about fifteen minutes to eleven. I started to investigate.

"Yes," said someone close to the mayor, "there was a shooting. If you want, I can give you the mayor's number."

"Sure, great, give me the mayor's number." So then I called the mayor and he told me:

"No, nothing is happening. Anyway, those *ayotzinapos* only come to make trouble. I was at my wife's annual report, she's the president of the DIF," and later we'd learn that she was about to launch her mayoral campaign. Then the mayor said that there were about seven thousand people at the event at one point. But that, due to the students' supposed shenanigans, only about a hundred stayed behind. He said he had stayed there to dance. So I then repeated my question, but he said:

"No, man, nothing is going on. Everything is fine. No one is injured; no one has been killed. Peace reigns here in Iguala."

ALEX ROJAS, FRESHMAN. We came from Periférico Sur. The bus driver told us: "Sure, kids, I know that you all do this every year and it's no big deal. Let's go. I've got family in Tixtla, but I work here. I want to go for a visit, too. Let's go, we'll head over there right now." The driver seemed eager to take us. We were all talking. We called back to the school to let them know we were on our way back. There were fourteen of us students on that bus, thirteen freshmen and one guy from the committee. So we called and said that we were on our way on an Estrella Roja bus, that we'd be there soon, and that the other buses were behind us somewhere, they had gotten held up a bit. We were driving along Periférico Sur, coming up to the last overpass before heading out of town toward Chilpancingo, when we saw that right beneath the overpass there was an Estrella de Oro bus. There were a bunch of police trucks both in front of the bus and behind it, you could see their siren lights in the distance. We could tell that the bus was an Estrella de Oro because we came within a hundred or a hundred and fifty meters to it at most, before stopping. The bus driver was trying to turn around when, just like that, a police car pulled up. The police made the driver get off the bus and detained him. We also got off the bus.

The police started arguing with us using obscene words.

"What the fuck are you all doing here? Get the fuck out of here or you'll all be dead."

"What of it? We can be here, we're not doing anything wrong."

And they started getting into it when the *compa* from the committee said:

"Come on, let's go, let's go!" Because there were so many police trucks surrounding the Estrella de Oro, they had it surrounded under the overpass, and so we walked about three blocks in the opposite direction.

ÓSCAR LÓPEZ HERNÁNDEZ, 18, FRESHMAN. Along Periférico Sur, I think. That's the route we took. And right at the overpass there was an Estrella de Oro and some state police—no, no, they weren't state police. I don't know. Maybe they were municipal police. I don't know what they were. Men with guns. They were already in the bus. The bus was completely surrounded. The police—there were about five police trucks—were all around the bus aiming their guns at it. It was dark. You could only see the siren lights and the police with their flashlights. But we couldn't see more because right then the police pulled up to where we were and aimed their guns at us. They told us to all get off the bus. We didn't see anything else that was happening with the Estrella de Oro bus because the police also stopped us at gunpoint there near the overpass. The guy from the committee shouted to us to grab some rocks. We grabbed some rocks and started arguing with the police so they would let us go.

The cops ordered us to drop the stones. They started bullying us, insulting us, and then fired a shot in the air. When they fired the shot, we took off running.

SANTIAGO FLORES, 24, FRESHMAN. So we all squeezed together in the space between the two buses. My lung had collapsed before. I had that medical history. And since we were all bunched together, there was a moment when we all fell down. I didn't feel anything when I fell, and couple of others fell on top of me, on my back. I remember that the *compa Chilango*, the Mexico City kid whose face they cut off, was with me. He was next to me and both of us were trying to take cover. Each time the others would push us a little, we'd get closer to the edge, closer to the edge. At one point we were stuck right at the very edge of the bus and if they'd pushed us just a bit we would have been exposed. So *Chilango* would push back to give us some room, but then they'd push against him again, and there we were. And then I started to. . . . I don't know what it was, the fear, all the pushing, or just all of it, but I started having trouble breathing. I couldn't breathe. I remember that I said to my *compas* that I couldn't breathe. I told *Chupa*, Drinker, the guy they call *Chupa* who was one of my roommates, I told him I couldn't breathe.

"Hold on, hold on," he said, "okay, now, sit down, sit down."

Everyone bunched together without sticking out from behind the buses, and they told me to sit down. There were about fifteen of us, more or less, maybe eighteen of us there. I sat down. I started to feel pain, here in my back, it started to go numb there. I couldn't get the air in and out of my lungs, like I wasn't breathing. I tried to breathe through my mouth and the *compas* told me to hold on. They took off the T-shirt I had wrapped over my face and several *compas* started fanning me, giving me air. Some of the *compas* were saying to call an ambulance and shouted out to the cops to call another ambulance because another student was down.

And, you know, during all this, the shootings kept on happening. I was sitting there leaning against the bus and thinking, well, it's one or the other, either they shoot me or I'm going to collapse here, one of the two. From where I was sitting I could see the police officer aiming at me from behind a light post. It seemed like they were pointing at you and they fired at you but then the bullet went some other way. I remember that I was ducked down and looking out at two cops, and I could see that they were aiming at me but I don't know if when they fired they pointed off in another direction. At one point I couldn't breathe well and the *compas* laid me down. They put some T-shirts here like a pillow and they said to the cops not to be assholes, to call another ambulance, and that they had already killed one of us, why do they want to kill another?

"We don't have any guns," I heard them shouting, "we just have rocks, we can only defend ourselves with rocks." But they stuck out their hands to show that they didn't even have any rocks and they said, "We're unarmed." The ambulance took a long time to arrive. One *compa* that was with me, they call him *Dedos*, Fingers, was trying to keep my spirits up, telling me to hold on. I remember that I squeezed his hand and said that we'd both stay strong.

"We'll get out of this," he told me, "don't give up, we'll make it." I squeezed his hand and said:

"But I can't really breathe, I don't know if I'll make it, I don't know."

A number of the *compas* that were there with us, we were crying, because, facing it, we knew what was going to happen. I told them that I wasn't going to make it and they told me no, I needed to hold on, that it wasn't over yet. I remember them carrying me. They told the cops:

"If you won't bring your truck, we'll carry him out

and you all take him." But right when they were going to, when they were going to carry me over to the police, the cops started shooting at us. The police wouldn't let them carry me out. They started shooting at us, and the *compas* screamed out to them not to be such assholes.

"Don't be shits, another student is sick, we just want you all to take him to a hospital, that's it, if not, he's going to die here." Then I heard the police shout that they'd only take one student. So they carried me out just a bit and left me there. A cop grabbed me and dragged me, he grabbed me by the hair and dragged me. He took me around the corner and threw me down. I fell face up. I couldn't breathe. The cop asked me what was wrong and said stuff like:

"See what happens? You knew what would happen."

"No, I didn't know." How the hell would one know this would happen?

When I was lying on the ground there I could see the police with their guns, the same police that had been aiming at me, they were screaming to the *compas* that they were fucked, that why had they come?

"Shoot 'em! Shoot 'em! Don't stop shooting at them! Why do they come here? So that we can teach them not to be such fucking idiots."

The police grabbed me by the feet and hands and threw me in the bed of the squad pickup. I thought: "Where are they taking me? The hospital?" And then they took off, flooring it, like there was no one in the back, as if I wasn't there. They took off like that, flooring it. And when they went over speed bumps, or braked, it was the same, and I was smashing around with a bunch of tubes they had in the bed of the truck. They went about two blocks. Since I didn't see any ambulance or anything, the street was abandoned, I thought: "I guess this is it, because I don't see any ambulance."

When I had been back there on the ground I had heard someone say, "The ambulance is here," but they didn't put me in an ambulance; they put me in their truck. And after about two blocks I thought to myself: "These cops aren't taking me to a hospital, not like they're driving, surely they're taking me somewhere else, who knows?"

It had been about three blocks when they slammed on the brakes. They braked and I went smashing around amid the tubes again and I thought: "Okay, now what?" And then there were some. . . . I don't know, paramedics, I don't know. They had a stretcher. The cops didn't say anything. And the others they just took me out of the truck and moved away. The cops didn't ask them anything, where they were taking me, nothing.

I didn't think that they would disappear me, because none of us thought about that. "They're arresting me," I thought to myself, "but they're not taking me to the hospital, because the way they dragged me along, the way they drove, that's not the way. . . . I mean, I'm kind of like dying, that's not the way to treat me, flying around in the bed of a pickup truck with a bunch of tubes."

The cops didn't even get out of their truck. The ones who came for me were the nurses, the paramedics. They then lifted my shirt up and immediately asked me what was wrong. They realized that I couldn't respond and then put an oxygen mask on me and put me in the ambulance.

"Breathe normally," they said, "otherwise you're just going to make it worse."

"But I can't, I can't." That was the only thing I could manage to say. And perhaps they couldn't understand me since I couldn't breathe. I spoke but it was like the words, like I couldn't pronounce them well. I don't know if they understood me.

JOSÉ ARMANDO, 20, FRESHMAN. We could see how they pulled the *compañeros* off the third bus. They kicked them and beat them as they stepped off the bus. The *compañero* who got shot in the hand was on that bus. They beat him as well. And we could see how the police took them to the squad trucks. The municipal police drove off with them.

JORGE, 20, FRESHMAN. After a while we heard them screaming. There was a little shop there and I saw a cop when he was throwing a *compañero* to the ground and then beating him and others once they were on the ground. And when the police took them, they made them keep their hands behind their heads. The police put them all in the squad trucks. I peeked through a window and could see where the police were putting several *compañeros* in the trucks and then took them away. I looked through the window quickly, because we could also see that in front of us two police kept aiming at us from behind a light post. That's why we only looked quickly through the windows, because we thought that if we didn't move away from the windows quickly then those two police would shoot us.

COYUCO BARRIENTOS, 21, FRESHMAN. We were all bunched together toward the back of the first bus, by the bathroom. Where I was taking cover, the window was broken, all cracked, with just one hole. I wanted to peek out through there to see if we could get out yet. But there were two police still aiming at us from behind, near the third bus. I could see that the police had some *compañeros* lying face-down on the ground. They had arrested them. And they were taking them inside some building. And they were still aiming at us, and shooting. The *compañeros* who were stuck between the two buses would shout out to the police that we were students, that we were unarmed, and that we didn't even have any more rocks: "We're unarmed!" But instead of talking or negotiating with us, they just kept shooting. Whenever the *compañeros* tried to videorecord the police, the cops would shine a flashlight at the *compañeros'* cell phones to make it impossible to see the cops' faces, to keep from being filmed.

IVÁN CISNEROS, 19, SOPHOMORE. We saw it when the police forced the students off the third bus and made them lie facedown on the ground with their hands like this, behind their heads. A bunch of them weren't wearing their T-shirts and the police made them lie down like that on the ground. And there we were watching, feeling powerless, angry. We couldn't do anything. We thought it was strange when they started putting the *compañeros* into the backs of the police squad trucks: they started to pick up all the spent bullet casings and clean the blood off the ground. Then a cop came up and said to us:

"Okay, leave now, get in your bus and leave." The driver got in the Costa Line that was in front and started the motor. We told him no, leave the bus where it is, don't move it. We were afraid that if he moved it the police would come for us. We screamed:

"No!" A *compañero* ran into the bus and grabbed the keys away from the driver. And so we stayed there a bit longer.

URIEL ALONSO SOLÍS, 19, SOPHOMORE. A bit later three big police trucks arrived. They were also municipal police, but the color of their squad trucks was different. It was a bright marine blue. A normal Iguala police truck is a Ranger with a double cabin. And the ones that arrived later were the really big Ram trucks. But they were municipal police. And they got out of their trucks dressed all in black, with gloves and ski masks and the municipal police shields. One of them got out and said:

"Let's negotiate." We told him to take off his ski mask if he wanted to talk with us. So he took it off and walked closer. He had short, frizzy hair, ragged eyelashes, and a mustache. He was tall with slightly dark skin. He told us to turn ourselves in.

"Alright guys," he said, "let's make a deal. You all are going to turn yourselves in. We're going to take the buses. We're going to pick up the bullet shells, and we'll act like nothing happened here." But no, that couldn't be. They had already shot a *compañero*. And they had arrested the other *compas*.

"No," we told him, "our *compañeros* are on their way. We're staying here."

"If you don't leave," he said, "you'll regret having come to Iguala for the rest of your lives. If you don't leave, we'll be coming back for you later." And then he left. He signaled for the rest of the police to leave. That was when the police started to get back in their trucks. They got the truck that was all smashed and shot up and took it too. They took everything, even the cars back behind the buses where they had arrested the *compañeros*.

We saw how they forced the *compañeros* from the third bus into their trucks and took them. They all left. When I first saw what was going on back there, I saw the *compañeros* all lying facedown on the ground. And the bus driver was there. It was hard, because whenever we tried to peek around the edge of the bus the police would shoot at us. So we would take shelter back behind the bus and couldn't see much. But we could see how the police had all the *compañeros* facedown on the ground. We thought that we'd all be arrested. That's what I was telling the freshmen, not to get bummed out, that the *compas* would be arrested and probably released the following day.

We stayed put. The cops left. And then cars started to circulate again. Before that no cars passed by at all. The streets were desolate. People started to come up and ask us what had happened and we told them. We started putting a bunch of rocks around the bullet shells so we could take photos of them and register the evidence. The seats on the third bus were covered in blood. The *compa* Bernardo's ID was covered in blood. The bus's tires were blown out and the windshield was covered in blood. We didn't know what the police had done to them. Our *compañeros* from the school arrived as well as some local Iguala teachers to offer help. We called the press. We thought that if the press arrived we'd feel safer.

CARLOS MARTÍNEZ, 21, SOPHOMORE. A police officer came up to talk to us. He started telling us to turn ourselves in, to throw out our weapons, and who knows what else, that we were screwed. He wanted someone to come out and tell him what had gone down, what happened. Well, we said:

"Fuck that. If you take one of us, you'll have to take us all. So if you really want us, come get us." But no, they didn't.

ERNESTO GUERRERO, 23, FRESHMAN. They started telling us: "Ok, assholes, you're all going to leave. Get on your bus and leave, otherwise you'll hear from us." But how were we supposed to leave if the bus was all shot up? We decided to stay because people from various organizations, from the CETEG teachers union, from here at the college, were on their way. And just to give you an idea, about an hour and a half after the police started shooting at us, our *compañeros* from the school arrived.

In that same hour and a half, did the army arrive, even though their base is located just meters away from where we were attacked? Not a single soldier came: nor the state police, nor state detectives, nor the army, nor the federal police, nor the marines. How we would have liked to see all those uniforms that are always in the streets intimidating people! But no, not even with a military base just meters away from where the police attacked us and shot at us.

We were there for about an hour or so when our *compañeros* from here at Ayotzinapa arrived in Iguala. Reporters from Morelos state showed up, but not a single detective honored us with an appearance, nor did anyone from the army. Someone told me that there was a detective on the way. And I went about looking for bullet shells. The municipal police picked up their bullet shells after firing, but even so they left several of them, including an unfired bullet. I told the reporters to take photographs of the evidence, and they did. I put marks around the shells so that when the detectives arrived, supposedly, they could find the shells easily. We students tried to cordon off the area and protect it as best we could. We put rocks and sticks around the bullet shells and other evidence so that no one would pick them up or step on them, so when the detectives arrived. . . . But they never came. An hour and a half went by, if not more, and they never showed up.

COYUCO BARRIENTOS, 21, FRESHMAN. When I didn't see any more movement outside I went up toward the front of the bus. From there I couldn't see anything either. Then some police passed by in front of the bus and I threw myself back down between the seats. They had seen us. They walked up to the door, but didn't get on the bus. We were all just waiting for the moment when it would be our turn to get the shit kicked out of us. But the police stayed over on the street corner. They weren't shooting anymore. When they started leaving, I think that was when they also drove off with the *compañeros* from the third bus. Those of us inside the first bus were still just waiting for it to be our turn. But then the police all started leaving. Then we didn't hear anything. Everything went quiet. The street was calm, in silence. And we saw that some guys were passing by on motorcycles. They seemed to be just passing by, looking around to see what had happened. We asked them if there were still police around. They said no. We asked them if they could check in front of the bus, and they did, they did us that favor and said that there was no one there.

That was when we started to get off the bus. We all met up between the two buses. We got together and checked to see who was injured, who was okay, who was missing. We talked about what had happened and where the others could be. We went to look through the other buses. Some students stayed back to keep watch at the street corners. We saw all the bullet shells on the ground. And the police had picked up a lot of the shells trying to cover up what they had done. We agreed not to move a single shell. That instead of moving them we would put some kind of marker around them like a rock so we could protect the evidence.

The *compañeros* were taking photos and filming. Some people started to arrive, including some parents, but they started to walk all over the evidence. So we made a human chain to protect the area. More people started to come. Someone called the local media in Iguala, but some of the journalists said they didn't have permission to report on the story. So reporters from Chilpancingo started to arrive. And a few local reporters managed to show up. A bit later the *compañeros* from Ayotzinapa who had come to help us arrived. They came in an Urvan. And some others came. At that moment we didn't know anything about what had happened to the students in the other two buses. We all started to talk. What's going on here? Are you okay? Is anyone else wounded? We started to talk about everything that had just happened and about the *compañeros* that the police had arrested. There was a lot of blood in the third bus. That bus was all torn up, all destroyed. We didn't know where the drivers had gone. We started to look for information about the *compañeros* the police had taken, about the different police squad trucks that were there during the attacks.

The press arrived and started gathering information. Some *compañeros* went looking for all the cell phone videos to gather them together. Everyone was still scared. No one had expected this. Sure, we all talked about how at the moment of truth we'd all fight back, but fight back with fists. No one had imagined that something like that could happen, and least of all from the municipal police. Something that I thought was really strange was that, when the police were still there, a squad truck arrived that looked just like a federal police truck in every way. But it had the "M" from "municipal" on the door. I couldn't see the tailgate. But it said POLICE and had the national symbol and the "M" from "municipal." But it was identical to a federal police truck. The police that came in that truck all wore masks like the feds. When that truck arrived all the other police had like a meeting, and then left. That seemed strange to me. I didn't understand that. In my opinion, it would seem that those were the *sicarios*, the hit men.

Since we were all gathered together, we started to check in with everyone there in order to try and lift our spirits. I was with my cousin, Daniel Solís. Well, he's not really my actual cousin, but a friend. I'm a friend of the family. I'd met him years before, before coming here to the college. And then here at the school our friendship, our brotherhood, got much stronger. We were always together. We did everything together. Before we came here his family had asked me to take care of him, since I'm a bit older.

PEDRO RENTERÍA LUJANO, 60, FOUNDER AND TECHNICAL DIRECTOR OF THE THIRD DIVISION SOCCER TEAM THE AVISPONES (HORNETS) OF CHILPANCINGO, GUERRERO. It was precisely that day, September 26, that we began the 2014–2015 third division soccer season. At eight-thirty that night we played against Iguala. The game ended. We won 3-1. After the game, a former player I had coached came up to say hello, and at that very moment got a call: he shouldn't go back to his neighborhood because there were gunshots. When he told me that, I said:

"You know what? We'd better get going. It's better we leave, because I've got all these kids, a lot of kids with me, and we don't want them to get hurt."

We left Iguala, or rather, we tried to leave but couldn't get on the fast lane precisely because they were attacking young people there. It took us about ten minutes to get on the highway. Then, after we got in the fast lane to get on the highway toward Chilpancingo, we were stopped for about ten minutes. On the outskirts of Iguala there was a police roadblock. They pulled the car ahead of us aside and let us through. We kept going. There was some roadwork about five kilometers outside of Iguala; traffic was reduced to one lane and we were stuck there for another while. There the bus driver asked the driver of another bus what was going on. That other driver said:

"Nothing, everything's okay," and so we kept going.

About ten kilometers on the way from Iguala toward Chilpancingo, at about ten minutes before the stroke of midnight would end the twenty-sixth, we started hearing bursts of machine-gun bullets striking the bus. Hearing the shots, the bullets, I shouted to the boys:

"Gunshots! Get down on the floor!" And that is what all of us, without exception, did. But in the gunfire we received from both the right and left sides of the bus, a shot hit the driver: a bullet hit him behind the ear and lodged in his brain. He lost control of the bus. He let go of the steering wheel and the bus went about thirty meters from where they shot us and came to a rest about ten meters off the road, tilting into a ditch.

When the bus came to a stop we were in front of the men who had been shooting at us from the right side; they began shooting at us from straight on. That's where they hit me twice: one bullet went into my abdomen, and the other into my liver. And they hit our physical trainer: one bullet grazed his eye and pierced his nasal septum, and the other bullet broke his left arm. One of the gunmen had his face covered, but the other one didn't. They were not wearing police uniforms. I only saw two of them, but there were definitely more than ten of them, easy. Taking into account the machine-gun bursts they fired at us, let's say there were eight on one side and eight on the other side, something like that. They shouted at us to open the door. The only one of us who got up was the physical trainer. He screamed out to them:

"We're a soccer team!"

They responded: "Open the door you son of a bitch!"

"I can't, I can't! You left me blind," the trainer said, "I've got a gunshot in my eye! I can't see!"

But even so, he did try to open the door, but it was stuck. So the gunmen started to strike the windshield and the door windows with their rifle butts to try to get inside. Luckily . . . I don't know what happened, if it was God's protection, if it was because we were all quiet, speechless, and they thought they'd killed us all, or if it was because the trainer had told them we were a soccer team, I don't know what it was that made them stop shooting at us, made them decide not to come on board and massacre us. They went off running straight into the darkness. All I could see, just barely, was the reflections from the lights on one of their trucks that they had left with the motor running and the lights on. They went running, shooting at the cars on the highway. Those poor people screamed as the bullets hit their cars. The killers left.

After that we all tried to get off the bus. We started climbing out through the broken windows, because that was the only way out. Some tried to ask for help on the highway, for someone to take the wounded to the hospital in Iguala: fifteen of us had been shot, out of the twenty-two aboard the bus. The amount of damage we took from the shooting, in my opinion, was minimal, because when they shot at us through the windshield that's when they hit everyone and that's when they killed one of the players, David Josué García Evangelista. He was in the aisle and raised his head; the bullet went through his neck. The team's doctor helped us take care of the wounded boys. We got out of the bus, but the federal police and the ambulances took a long time to give us help. They got to us around ten minutes before two in the morning, and we were only a ten-minute drive from Iguala. They didn't want to help us. I called the president of the team we played against in Iguala, Humberto Chong Soto.

"They shot us," I said, "there are a bunch of wounded people, probably a few people killed, please send me ambulances."

"I'll send them right away," he said.

But later I was able to speak with him and he told me that the ambulances didn't want to go, they were afraid to go out there to where we'd been shot. So, that led to us spending so much time out there wounded and bleeding. The ambulances took me and several of the boys to the hospital at around two in the morning. We arrived at the Iguala General Hospital and that was where they operated on us. They started operating on me at around three in the morning. The operation lasted until six in the morning, and I was in intensive care for twelve days. After they discharged me from the hospital, I came back home to Chilpancingo to continue treatment and rehabilitation. Now, on doctor's orders, I can walk and jog.

FACUNDO SERRANO URIOSTEGUI, 41, CHILPAN-CINGO MUNICIPAL SPORTS DIRECTOR. We left at a quarter to eleven. The game went from eight to ten. We played both halves. The final score was 3-1 in favor of the Avispones. The players then went to the locker rooms to change and we were waiting for the referees to finish the game certificate and give it to us. That took about half an hour or forty minutes. By the time the boys had changed and the referees gave us the certificate, it was about ten-forty.

We got on the bus. Since we had traveled to Iguala earlier that day and we hadn't had any rest, we were all a bit tired. As soon as we got on the road, the driver put on a movie. We were all seated, watching the TV, with the curtains all drawn. We were watching the movie. We were tired; some people were sleeping. All of a sudden we felt the glass and heard shots. Some people were hit immediately. The bus went off the road and came to a stop, leaning to the right. All the bullet shells were out on the highway. They had been waiting for us. We screamed:

"We're soccer players!" The gunmen wanted to board the bus, but they couldn't open the door. They said:

"You fuckers are dead!"

One of the physical trainers, Jorge León Sáenz, screamed that we were a soccer team, pleaded with them to stop shooting, that there were minors, children on the bus. To which they responded that they didn't give a fuck, and that we were as good as dead. They shot us again, thinking, obviously, that we were Ayotzinapa students. When they realized that we weren't the people they were looking for, they said:

"Now we've fucked up." Literally, those exact words, they said: "Commander, we fucked up, they're soccer players." Then they went back to their cars. We heard more shots, because they attacked a car that was behind us and another person died.

We realized that one boy was severely wounded. The doctor went to look at him when, after five or six minutes, he stopped breathing and ceased to exist. There were three of us adults taking care of the wounded. After we had done some first aid, a federal police patrol car arrived. That was about forty minutes after the attack. But the police didn't want to help us. One of the feds took out his cell phone and asked:

"How many dead, how many wounded?"

"We want you to help us, not interview us!"

"Just wait a bit, an ambulance is on the way."

"Let us use your patrol car; we must get the wounded to a hospital."

We were going to start putting the wounded in his patrol car.

"I dare you to put him in my car. I dare you," the cop said.

"Can't you see us?! They attacked us! What we want is help."

And still the cops said they went to help us. . . .

CLEMENTE AGUIRRE, 38, PHYSICAL TRAINER FOR THE AVISPONES. We knew that something was happening in the center of Iguala. We were trying to decide whether or not to get dinner in Iguala or Chilpancingo. The boys wanted to celebrate. They wanted to get tacos.

"Let's eat here," they said.

"No, let's head back to Chilpancingo. We can get dinner there," we said. Once we were on the highway we were all really caught up in the movie *Now You See Me*. Everything was really shocking, really fast. At first the shots sounded like they were part of the movie, or like firecrackers. The bus kept moving. The first thing I thought was that they were going to come for us. And I managed to say out loud:

"Kids, keep quiet, don't make a sound." But they started groaning with pain. And indeed, the gunmen came up to the bus and told us to open up and get off the bus. Another *compañero* started to say:

"Easy, brother, we're a soccer team."

"Get out of the bus, bitches!"

"Take it easy, brother. We're a soccer team!"

"You're not getting off then? Get the fuck off!"

So they tried to open the door, but it was jammed; it wouldn't open. So they shot at the door. We didn't move. We stayed down on the floor. We just waited. It was impossible to know if they would get on the bus or not. I thought: "If they get on the bus, we're done." But as far as us getting off: no way. I wasn't going to move an inch. They screamed:

"Now you all are fucked!" They shot at us again. It wasn't much, a little, I don't know, maybe ten seconds. They stopped shooting and they left. But we stayed still, nobody moved. After a bit we started to lift ourselves up and climb out through the busted windows on both sides of the bus. When we started to get off the bus, some of the boys took off running, about fifteen of them, pretty much all the boys. They were hiding in the cornfields for a long time, until the ambulances started arriving. We started getting the wounded people off the bus. I pulled out my phone and immediately called for an ambulance. But that ambulance never arrived. I was thinking the attackers might return. And with that thought, I wanted someone to send the police, ambulances, something. No cars passed by on the road for almost half an hour, but even then, none wanted to stop. We screamed out to them:

"Help!" But they just went slow enough to get a good look and then floored it. We were all covered in blood. The most seriously wounded ones were the bus driver, Coach Pedro, and Miguel. The rest, from all the adrenaline, didn't even feel their wounds, like Facundo with all the shrapnel in his chest.

The police and the ambulances took about an hour and

a half to arrive. But first, actually, a car did stop, a car with some people from Mexico City, *chilangos*, who wanted to help. I was with the bus driver. The car stopped and two young women came up, held the driver's head in their hands so that he wouldn't choke on his blood. They tried to take care of him. The police arrived and I thought: "Okay, now it'll be okay." We said:

"Let's get the wounded in the squad cars." So me and some others, including one of the *chilangos*, went to take Coach Pedro, who had multiple gunshot wounds, to the police car. We lifted him, carried him, and sat him in a police car.

"Sit him there in the meantime," the police officer gave us permission. And then we went for Miguel, we lifted him, and when we were going to put him in the other police car, the cop said:

"Don't even think about putting him in my car." One of the guys helping said:

"But he's seriously wounded, we can't just leave him like this. We have to get him to a hospital." The cop said:

"Nope, you're not putting him in my car. The ambulance is on the way." I was holding Miguel by the butt and legs; the other guy was holding him by the arms. We had to set him down on the ground, next to the squad car.

ALEX ROJAS, FRESHMAN. What I'm going to tell you is rarely mentioned in the news. In the news you only heard about the shootings by the mini Aurrera, off of Periférico Norte, but we had a different problem. There were fourteen of us who took the Periférico Sur route out of the bus station. And yes, when we were stopped we went back about three blocks and then ran, because we know that the police can be jerks sometimes, that's how they are, assholes. We ran and then hid in the woods. For about two hours we were wandering around in the woods, but we couldn't find any paths. Before that, when we were still on the Estrella Roja bus, we had heard that our *compañeros* were being shot at near the mini Aurrera. Someone there had called the *paisa* on the committee who was with us and told him they were under attack and a *compañero* had already been killed, but they hadn't identified him yet. We were worried about what was going on there and decided to go back to the mini Aurrera to help them. We ran a good way, but Iguala is big. We decided to wait for the two Urvans that were coming from the school to help. They were bringing sophomores, juniors, and the committee secretary general. They told us they'd look for us by the last overpass before leaving Iguala, the very overpass where the police had stopped the Estrella de Oro bus. They said they'd pick us up there. We went back and crossed over the bridge in groups of four because there were so many police right beneath us. We crossed over and the police didn't see us. We hid in a patch of woods on the other side of the overpass and waited there.

After hiding there a long time, we came down the curving ramp that goes down from the overpass to the Periférico. We went down and saw that all the police had left and the Estrella de Oro bus was abandoned there alone. For a second we thought about going over to see what was going on, or what had happened, but then we decided against it, thinking that there could be feds on board the bus, they might have set a trap for us, or something. Instead we decided to walk along the Periférico back toward the center of Iguala. We went walking all along the Periférico, thinking to offer help to our *compañeros*. And we went walking along the Periférico because the Urvans would have to pass by at some point.

We crossed over to the other side, facing oncoming traffic on the way out of town toward Chilpancingo, and we saw one of the Urvans driving on the other side, toward Iguala, but they didn't see us. So the Urvans had already passed on their way to help out where the shootings had occurred.

We kept walking, and walking, and then ran because two municipal police squad trucks had seen us. We had heard that the police had killed one of our *compañeros*, and yeah, we screamed at the police to go away. But the two police trucks kept following behind us. No one got out of the trucks. They just stayed back there, following us a good way. Then two more police trucks came and right then, two state government civil protection trucks went by and then turned around to come back and face us. The two civil protection trucks came right up to us and then put their trucks in reverse. And behind us there were four municipal police trucks. We were walking in the middle. And then three more police trucks pulled up behind the civil protection trucks and stopped, forcing those two trucks to stop as well. And we were stuck between all those police, in the middle of the street.

There were three police trucks and two civil protection trucks in front of us and another four police trucks behind us. You know, that's a lot of police. There were fourteen of us students, with nothing. We had just been walking. And then the police all got out of their trucks. I thought . . . it passed through my mind that we were fucked. "They're going to arrest us," I thought. And since some older schoolmates had told us about getting arrested and how the cops overpower them and beat the crap out of them, I thought: "Okay, well, tough luck, this is as far as we can get." I thought they would arrest us and take us to jail after beating the shit out of us.

I thought: "Well, too bad, when they start beating us, we'll have to see what we can do." The police began approaching us, cocking and aiming their guns at us. I had a rock, and a couple of other *compañeros* did too. The police began shouting at us.

"Okay, listen here you motherfuckers! Drop your rocks now or you're all dead! You're all fucked, you stupid kids, you're fucked, you can't escape!"

"Okay then, do it, if you're gonna shoot, do it, you already hit one of us, you already killed one of our *compañeros*, you want another one, fucking do it!"

And they were aiming at us and coming closer. Luckily, behind us there was a little stream that had footbridges over it every ten meters or so. And just about three steps away, right behind us, there was a thin little wooden footbridge, about a meter wide. We crossed over that bridge without thinking. No one said a word. We just crossed the bridge and went over to the other side. We stayed there. Then the police started crossing the bridges and coming after us. Three more plainclothes police came after us. They picked up rocks and threw rocks at us. We threw the rocks we had back at them. There was a neighborhood behind us. We didn't even look. We ran up that way because the police were throwing rocks at us. We also fought back with our rocks. But then with only pavement all around, we didn't have any more rocks. So we ran.

There was a narrow street right behind us and we all ran down that street until we came to a path that went up a hill, the neighborhood was on a really steep hill. And there were steps, a shit ton of steps, going straight up. And we saw those steps, luckily we found them, and we all ran. And the police ran behind us. When we started running up the steps—they were really steep, almost like a staircase—some of the guys were almost running on all fours. We were racing with fear, you know. All those police trucks with their sirens. . . . And then when the police started running up the steps we heard gunshots. They started firing their weapons, and that made us all the more terrified. We kept going: running, running, running. We started screaming to each other.

"Faster! Hurry! Let's go! Don't fall behind!"

We were shouting and a woman up above, in a house, was screaming too.

"Leave them alone," she was saying. "Those boys aren't doing anything to you. They aren't doing anything! Leave them alone, they aren't doing anything, don't kill them!"

We ran up to the top where the woman's house was and we knocked on her door. We could still see the siren lights and everything down below. The police didn't run up into the neighborhood, they just shot at us. They only fired about five shots at us at that moment. And we asked the *tía* to let us hide there.

"*Tía*, open up, please let us come in." And she did. We went inside. She closed her doors and turned off her lights. But four of our *compañeros*—we were fourteen in total—had kept running, terrified, I guess. They kept running farther up the hill and went straight into the woods up there. They went in the woods and we couldn't see them. We began shouting out to them.

"*Paisa*, come back!" "*Chiquilín*, Tiny, come back!" We shouted out to them like that but they didn't care. They were really scared and kept running. We lost contact with them. We went inside the house. I told the *paisa* from the committee:

"If you want, I don't mind, I'll go look for them, I'll take the risk."

"No, no, no. Stay here. We can't risk you too."

"I don't mind. I'll go real quick."

"No, just stay here. We'll go look for them after sunrise. They'll be okay, they'll know how to hide too."

We stayed there. The *tía* asked us what we had been doing. We told her. Then she said: "Well, the police are always like that here, always patrolling, supposedly protecting." We stayed there. We wrote text messages with the *compañeros* in other parts of the city, the ones we had phone numbers for. We were all scared. It was about eleven or eleven-thirty, I think, when I sent a message to a *paisa* on the committee:

"*Paisa*, where are you? What's happening where you are?"

"Hide, don't separate," he responded, "they just came to shoot us again, hide, we'll regroup after sunrise." That was all he told me. Some of the students back at the school called me and sent me messages like this:

"*Paisa*, what's happening? *Compa*, how is everyone? How are you? What's going on? Do you have any info?" I answered some like this:

"I think they killed more *compañeros*, I don't know how many are dead, we're all spread out across different parts of Iguala, we're all hiding, we ran wherever we could." I wrote to one *compañero*:

"Honestly, I'm scared, truly, I don't know what is going to happen because the police are looking for us, they're patrolling around looking for us, we'll see what happens if they find us here." Some of the *compas* wrote back to me saying:

"Don't give up, they won't find you, hide, be careful, everything will be okay, in the morning it will be different, we're going to wait, we're going to go help you all, but we can't go right now."

They said they couldn't go then because apparently there were police roadblocks set up where the police wouldn't let any Ayotzinapa students through, they had orders to stop and arrest any kid from Ayotzi trying to go help in Iguala. A number of us were writing texts like that. The *tía* was also getting worried.

"I really don't want any trouble here," she said.

"*Tía*, we'll go by dawn, don't worry, nothing is going to happen here,"

We were lucky: We had a roof over our heads. Other *compañeros* were out in the woods. And it rained that night, a light rain, but rain nonetheless. And those out in the woods, in the brush, got all wet taking cover there.

JOSÉ, 18, FRESHMAN. Up ahead we could see municipal police trucks blocking the road. We got off the bus and started to grab rocks and the police officers started insulting us.

"You're all gonna die, you fucking animals."

One of them pointed his flashlight in our faces and then drew his pistol and pointed it at us. He was about six meters away and aiming straight at our chests.

"Why are you pointing your gun at us? Why are you aiming at us?"

Then we backed up. We saw that there were more police coming and took off running toward a hill. We ran off to the left, up a hill, and hid there for about two hours in an abandoned house. After that we went back down to the highway. We walked along the edge of the road and then we noticed that there were a number of police trucks nearby, and we ran back up the hill and then walked along a dirt road. We went over several hills and then went back down to the highway. There was a bridge there and we saw that there were still a number of police trucks beneath it, about ten or thirteen police trucks. They saw us and started to come after us, so we hid in some brush.

It started raining. We hid there for quite a while, about an hour. When the police left we decided to follow the highway. One of our *compañeros* called a member of the committee and asked where they were. So we started heading to a Bodega Aurrera, but we never got there. We were walking straight down the road when we saw two police trucks coming toward us. We were walking on the left side of the road and saw the two trucks coming at us. They were moving fast and the municipal police tried to hit us with their trucks. We were able to recognize one of the police officers then, a woman who is now under arrest. They did that twice. First they tried to run us over with one of the squad trucks, then a bit farther down the road they circled back and tried a second time. Both times we jumped up onto the sidewalk. It was a miracle they didn't kill us right there because they were really close when the driver jerked the wheel, and by pure reflex were jumped up on the sidewalk.

We kept walking and then we realized that there were about eight police trucks coming toward us. We ran about five hundred meters when the police and a truck from the public prosecutor's office all boxed us in. Seeing that we were trapped, we ran to the left, toward some houses, and started to defend ourselves against those eight truckloads of police and some state police too. They started throwing rocks at us, and we threw rocks back at them. And that's when the cops started shooting at us. We ran toward some alleys and then up some steps. We ran up like two hundred steps and when there were no more steps we kept running up a hillside. The police kept after us, shooting at us. We knew they were shooting to kill, because when they fired a few of us heard the bullets whizzing by, the screeching of the bullets cutting the air. We could hear that whistle of the bullets passing right by us. We kept running up the hill, and the police stopped following us but we kept running. We didn't stop for anything. Sometime around midnight, we were exhausted and stopped for a while. A woman let us stay on the patio outside of her house. We spent the night there.

CHAPARRO, 20, FRESHMAN. We were in the first bus that left the station. The driver asked us to give him a minute to stop and wait for someone to bring him some documents. He called the person, but they didn't show up to the place they said they would. He started the bus up again and asked that we give him another five minutes, that the person bringing him the documents was on their way. We were stopped there for maybe fifteen minutes. We were on our way out of town about to go under the overpass they call Santa María, though I'm not sure about that name. About then someone called the *compa* from the committee who was with us and told him that the municipal police had just killed one of our *compañeros*. The *compa* from the committee told the bus driver to turn around and go back quickly to where the attack was happening. The driver sped up, but when we were coming up to the overpass where we could veer off the highway and turn around we heard some *compas* say that some people were hijacking a bus. That seemed strange. Who was hijacking a bus? But then, coming a bit closer, we saw municipal and federal police trucks and cars. Both the feds and the local police were there. We didn't know if the people in the bus were our *compañeros* or someone else. Then two federal police cars pulled up with the cops aiming their guns at us, like they always do, and telling us to drop our rocks. We told them to lower their guns and turn off the flashlights they were shining in our faces. And we started arguing, you know, shouting insults and things like that at the police.

"Let us go, dickface!"

"No, you fucking assholes, drop your rocks."

"No. Take your fucking bus."

And then we turned around and calmly started walking away, back toward the center of Iguala. We walked about a kilometer, and then ran.

JUAN SALGADO, FRESHMAN. No authorities of any kind arrived to protect the crime scene. No state police arrived. No one whatsoever showed up to cordon off the area. We were the ones who, on our own initiative, were finding and marking the locations of the bullet shells. We put rocks around them, or a cup over them so that no one would move them, treating them like evidence. Some students started taking photos. Since we saw that no one was showing up, we said we'd have to cordon off and protect the area as best we can. After a bit, some reporters started to arrive. The *compañeros* from the school also arrived. Two Urvans from the school arrived. I don't know exactly how many *compañeros* came, but some did show up.

"What happened? How is everyone?"

"We're okay."

"And the others?"

"They took some *compañeros*."

"How many did they take?"

"Between fifteen and seventeen. They took them off in their police trucks."

"But you guys are okay?"

"Yes, but two guys are wounded."

"And the others who are wounded?"

"They took them to the hospital."

And, well, there we were answering a thousand questions, doing interviews. At that point a junior from the college gave us a cigarette and said: "Have a smoke to calm your nerves, because its obvious you guys are freaked out." And so we sat down on the curb.

GERMÁN, 19, FRESHMAN. We were there for a while. People started taking pictures. I think the press showed up, or something like that, I'm not sure. People were taking pictures of the bullet holes, the empty shells, and the blood from the *compa* who got hit. I was talking to my girlfriend on the phone. I was telling her that it was all over, it was calmer and that the police had left. That's why I stepped away from the group where everyone had gathered. I told them that I was going to make a call. There were about five or six *compas* there with me. We were keeping watch over the avenue. I was talking with my girlfriend when I heard that someone was shooting at us again. I didn't see them, because I was far from them, almost at the other edge of the road, far. I heard the shots. I didn't turn around to look, but started running and running. I hung up on my girlfriend, because she could hear the shots too. There was a young woman among the people I was running with, a young woman who belonged to some kind of an organization there in Iguala. She knew the city and took us to a house. We hid there. My girlfriend called me but I didn't answer. I sent her a message that I couldn't talk because we were hiding in silence, trying not to make any noise.

"I'm okay," I wrote to her, "thank God. I'll call you, don't worry."

JORGE HERNÁNDEZ ESPINOSA, 20, FRESHMAN. We were standing on the street corner, near the buses. I was talking to a *compañero*, the one whose face they cut off, and he was telling me about everything that had happened, how they took our *compañeros* and everything. He was really freaked out, really nervous, scared, his voice would break as he spoke, like he was about to cry but, I don't know, like he was really scared.

"Nothing happened to you," I said to him.

"No. Luckily I was one of the people in the very back of the bus and just hid there when they started shooting at the bus."

He had hidden under the seats. So then, all of a sudden, this pickup drives by and takes our picture. Their camera flash went off. I asked *Chilango*:

"What's up with that guy?"

But we didn't pay it any further attention. We kept talking and a bit later I went over to the other side of the avenue and saw three men dressed in black, their faces covered, right when they began to shoot. I ran away, down the street, away from them. *Chilango* was running behind me.

JUAN RAMÍREZ, 28, FRESHMAN. The police left. I was walking around with a cousin. The press arrived. The reporters started to take photos, take notes on how many bullet shells there were and stuff like that. After this some *compañeros* bought cigarettes. We all started smoking. I was talking with the guy from Mexico City. But, with what happened later, well, he too . . . no one imagined. . . . He was telling me that the next day he was going to go home because he didn't want to risk his life. He was thinking about his family, his wife and daughter, and said that they were the most important things to him. All of a sudden I saw a black pickup truck. But I didn't see the people in it well. They started shooting in the air. And then they started shooting at us, and I forgot about the *compa* from Mexico City. I ran as fast as I could.

PEDRO CRUZ MENDOZA, IGUALA-BASED TEACH-ER, MEMBER OF THE STATE COORDINATION OF EDUCATION WORKERS OF GUERRERO (CETEG). I was in a meeting with other members of the CETEG. Around ten at night I got a message from a *compañera*. I called her and said:

"What's up?"

"Listen," she said, "they've just attacked the boys from Ayotzinapa. They killed someone! Get the others and come over here." And, well, since it is kind of common for the government to hurt the *compañeros* from Ayotzi, we immediately went over there. About twenty of us from the CETEG arrived little by little to help the students from Ayotzinapa. With a *compañera* we walked around taking pictures and trying to investigate what had happened. We spoke with a young man who told us he had been wounded: a bullet grazed him. We were trying to reconstruct the facts. The bus drivers were very shaken. A woman with a store nearby came out and offered the drivers some tequila, for their nerves.

"How much do we owe you for the bottle?"

"Keep the bottle, it's for you all; you seem really terrified," she said.

The drivers each took a shot of tequila. We called some other *compañeros* and they said that they had called the state detectives and that no one was there, absolutely no one.

When we arrived we didn't see the young man who had been shot in the head, but we did see a pool of blood and a T-shirt. A student there told us that the young man without a shirt on had put his shirt under the wounded guy's head to keep him from drowning in his own blood. And that was all they could do to help him, put a shirt under his head. Inside the buses we found a bunch of spent bullet casings on the floor and blood all over the seats. And since no detectives had arrived the students surrounded the casings with rocks to mark them.

"Be careful," they said, "there are some rocks over there, they're marking the bullet shells, please don't step on them or kick them."

Honestly, we were there for about an hour and a half, two hours trying to help the *compañeros* and waiting for the authorities. We arrived at around ten or ten-fifteen, sometime around then. And yeah, we were easily there for two hours and not a single authority showed up, eh? I asked the *compañeros* if they had called the press. They told me they had. But the reporters also took a while to arrive. They must have showed up around eleven or twelve that night.

Some of the reporters know me and came up to me. I was standing with my *compañeros* from the CETEG talking about what had happened. We were asking ourselves why those fiends had done this to the students. Just then a reporter approached me.

"Prof Pedro, can you give us any information?"

"No, I can't, the students have their political structure and specific people assigned to do that. They're over there, they're going to give a press conference."

A group of students and teachers from the CETEG were forming a circle near the corner with the Periférico. That's where we were when we heard. . . . I remember that I heard three shots—*bam-bam-bam!*—in rapid succession, like from a semi-automatic. And then came the machine-gun bursts. It was a complete strafing. We lost track of some of our *compañeras* standing by our side at that moment. Who knows which way they ran?

ANDRÉS HERNÁNDEZ, 21, FRESHMAN. So what I did was run and run. Since I know my way around Iguala, I shouted to my *compañeros* to follow me. But they were so terrified they split up and ran in all different directions. Before I knew it I was running by myself. I ran and ran—what was it?—about four or five blocks away from the shooters. I saw a taxi and signaled it to stop. I don't know if the taxi driver had realized what was happening, but he stopped and I got in without a dime in my pocket. I didn't have anything. I was wearing *huaraches*.[6] I asked him to take me to my aunt's house. She lives near the bus station for the Estrella Blanca line. The driver was very kind and took me. When we arrived he didn't charge me anything.

I was knocking on my aunt's door for half an hour. They were all asleep. I knocked and knocked; they woke up and let me in. I went inside and sat down. I still couldn't believe what I had just lived through. They spoke to me, but I don't know, I couldn't answer them. I was still in shock.

JORGE, 20, FRESHMAN. While we were just sitting there, suddenly we saw what looked like flames coming from the street. But they were gunshots. They were shooting at us again. There was a young woman with us where we were sitting. She couldn't run well, so we helped carry her. We

---

6. Handmade sandals

went running down some street. I don't know what its name is. But in every street corner the *compañeros* started dispersing. We weren't all running together. Some went a different way, but we kept going with the young woman. About two blocks farther down the street she directed us to a door and knocked. I don't know how she knew the woman at that house, but the woman let us in. She hid us there. She took us all into a room to hide. There were about fifteen of us.

URIEL ALONSO SOLÍS, 19, SOPHOMORE. Sometime around one in the morning on the twenty-seventh, a convoy of unmarked cars arrived: a red truck and some white cars. Men dressed in black, wearing face masks, with bulletproof vests, but without any government insignias on their clothes, got out of the vehicles. They were dressed in all black. By how they fired their weapons, we thought they were soldiers or paramilitaries. We saw some throw themselves down on the ground, others knelt down, and others stayed standing and they all started firing rifles. So we all ran. I got a look at about three of them. They were tall. They weren't wearing helmets, just vests, gloves, and face masks. They all had short hair like soldiers. And they were tall.

In that moment we all ran. Run or die. We all ran. The shots lasted a long time. They kept shooting for maybe five or ten minutes. I hid about three blocks from there in a field with three other *compañeros*. We stayed there. When we had just gotten to the field we heard something like if they had grabbed a *compañero*. Like a person being beaten, he screamed:

"Let me go!"

We said to each other that they must have grabbed a *compañero*. We saw police trucks drive by. It was a full-on hunt for students that night. Then it started raining. It rained and rained. We were hiding in the brush, in the dark. I called a couple of *compañeros* to ask how they were.

"We're up on a roof," one told me.

"We're in the hillside," others said.

"We're about three blocks away hiding in a woman's house," others answered.

They'd been lucky, the ones hiding in a house. We were really cold, and more than anything, afraid. We thought that if they found us there, they wouldn't just arrest us; we thought they would kill us. That's why we were so terrified, so scared.

RODRIGO MONTES, 32, JOURNALIST FROM IGUA-LA. I got there at around eleven-thirty. The buses had bullet holes everywhere. You could see that the police had shot at them from all angles. There were bullet holes in the windshields, the windows, the tires, the sides, I mean, everywhere. The third bus, the last one in line, that was where a lot of students had been riding; the others told us that they had felt safer there. And that was where the police had forced them off the bus. There were several pools of blood on that bus. That's where the police grabbed the majority of the students. They spoke of between twenty-five and thirty students taken from that bus. There were AR-15 and nine-millimeter bullet shells inside the bus.

There was a period of hours during which nothing happened. No authorities arrived at any point. Nobody. When I got there, around eleven-thirty, no authorities were present. The area hadn't been cordoned off. There were no soldiers, no detectives, no police, nobody. Absolutely nobody from the government, not a soul. But more students from the college had arrived. There were about fifty people there between students, teachers from the CETEG, and journalists. There were six of us reporters there during the press conference. Precisely when they were finishing the press conference, as the students who had spoken were telling us their names, we heard the gunfire. They were machine-gun bursts: an infinity of gunshots.

At first we thought they were shooting in the air. But when we starting hearing the projectiles—you can hear it when the bullets pass by you, this whizzing sound—and the car windows shattering, then we all began running toward the buses, down Álvarez street. A *compañero* and I took cover in the Aurrera parking lot.

The gunmen were shooting to kill. Imagine the terror and confusion that caused: the screaming, the cries of pain from those who had been wounded. It was chaos. It was really very terrifying. It seemed to go on for fifteen minutes, but no, actually, the shooting lasted three minutes tops. But you feel that time like an eternity. The machine-gun bursts sounded like they came from high-caliber weapons. I left at around one or one-fifteen and no authorities had yet arrived. The gunmen had all the time in the world to do whatever they wanted. No authorities ever showed up.

GABRIELA NAVALES, 28, JOURNALIST FROM IGUALA. Around eleven-thirty that night I got a call from a teacher named Erika. She said:

"Hello, this is Erika from the CETEG and I'd like you to attend a press conference at the corner of Álvarez and Periférico about the attack on the Ayotzinapa students." I told her I'd go. I called another reporter and asked him to check whether it was true or not that there had been a shooting with several people wounded and killed. He looked into it and then told me that yes, it was true, and there was going to be a press conference in a few minutes. I went with my husband and my boss from the newspaper. We arrived and saw an Urvan and a number of cars blocking the road, and then there were the buses. There were three buses in the middle of the street. The buses all had flat tires and bullet holes all over them. The students told us to go on the buses to take photographs to prove what they had suffered at the hands of the municipal police. We went to take the photos. There was blood on the bus, and a student's ID card. We found rocks of all different sizes. We got off the bus and the students asked us to wait for a few minutes, for more reporters to arrive before beginning the press conference. We waited. There were students standing on both sides of the corner of Álvarez and Periférico keeping watch. They said that more students had arrived from the school to help them.

We were waiting there for a while. At a few minutes after midnight we saw that the press conference was about to begin. We formed a kind of "U" around the students to be interviewed. One of the students started talking about the attack, saying that it was the municipal police. He started narrating the events. We had been listening for about two minutes when we heard the first shots. People began screaming:

"Take cover! Get down! They're shooting!" A number of students on my right side threw themselves to the ground. Others fell. Everyone ran toward the center of town. I stayed standing there, in shock. One of my sandals broke and I stayed right there while everyone ran.

One of the students screamed to me: "Take cover! Get down!" I didn't respond. Then one of the students pushed me and threw me to the ground. Everyone was screaming.

"On the ground! On the ground! Don't lift your head! On the ground!" I was listening to the screams, the gunshots, and the bursts of machine-gun fire. We all looked at each other down on the ground, confused, not knowing what to do or how to act. We didn't know who was attacking us nor from which direction the shots were coming.

I heard my husband's voice telling me to go with him. He pulled me down Álvarez Street, in the direction of the Cristina Clinic. We ran, and the gunshots continued. The shooting didn't stop. We took cover between the buses and the walls. We lost track of the other reporters and only saw students who were also running in every direction, all confused. When the shots stopped, we turned toward Juárez Street when my husband said:

"Here they come, here they come!" We saw two large trucks driving by at top speed. My husband pulled me in the other direction, toward Hidalgo Street. As we were crossing Álvarez again we came upon some students helping someone wounded and going toward the clinic. We kept going toward Hidalgo. On the corner of Hidalgo and Pacheco we saw four police officers calmly eating tacos. We stopped a taxi and left the area.

ERNESTO GUERRERO, 23, FRESHMAN. They shot us again. I was on the opposite corner talking with a friend when all of a sudden it sounded like a bunch of fireworks going off, like someone had thrown a pack of firecrackers into a fire: a horrible racket, a strafing, a rainstorm of bullets coming straight at us. When I looked back, I saw a crowd of people running in my direction. The reporters all came running. I even bumped into the TV reporter and said to him:

"Film this!" But he said: "No, man, they'll kill me!" He

got in his little car and took off. I was one of the last people to leave the area. There was a teacher standing on the corner. I asked her: "Aren't you going to leave?" She said: "I can't find my husband." She stayed there. I left. Everyone had run down Juan N. Álvarez. I got to a corner and turned with a group of *compañeros*, two reporters, two teachers, and a man. From there we went to a teacher's house.

COYUCO BARRIENTOS, 21, FRESHMAN. I was with my cousin and the other *compañero* who was killed. He was in the marching band with me. His nickname was *Fierro*, Iron, but also Pistol. We were there with another *compa* we call *Grande*, Big, and a *compa* we call *Sharpa*. We were starting to talk about what had just happened, if everyone was okay. What had happened? Next to us some of the *compañeros* who came from the school to help us were looking at cell phone videos. At that moment the general secretary of the committee was giving an interview, or a statement to the press.

I stepped away from my friends to turn back a taxi that was about to drive through the area. I saw that a white truck had driven by a number of times. It was a Lobo[7] with a radio antenna on the cab and someone riding in the back. They went by three times, more or less. I didn't see it go by a fourth time. After the third time a black car drove by, an Ikon or a Chevy. It went slowly by in front of us and a *compañero* saw that they took our photo. He even said:

"Hey, they took our picture with a flash!"

The strangest thing about that car was that it didn't pass by in the correct lane, but was driving really slowly the wrong way in the left-hand lane. After that car drove by the first *sicario* arrived. He started shooting in the air. Then

---

7. A Ford truck model.

they started shooting at us. I turned back and clearly saw the sparks of the bullets hitting the pavement, like Christmas firecrackers. The sparks flew from the pavement toward us. It seems like in a movie when they tell you that your life flashes before your eyes.

So what we did then was run. Then two other people got out of a car and started shooting at us. They were all dressed in black and wearing face masks. They were spraying us with machine-gun fire. They didn't pause for a moment. One of them was standing right in the middle of the street, another was beside him near the cars, and the other was up on the sidewalk, next to the wall of a building. They were just shooting at those of us in the road and everyone at the press conference. I ran as best as I could. I don't know how, but I made it over to some parked cars. A lot of students ran with us. Others ran toward the buses, or towards the Aurrera. Everyone ran off in different directions, and we didn't know where they went.

I didn't see where Daniel was. I was trusting, I was certain that he was safe, that he had been able to run. And those fucking assholes kept shooting. They didn't stop for a moment.

JORGE HERNÁNDEZ ESPINOSA, 20, FRESHMAN. I turned down the first cross street, and then turned again down the first street I came to; it was an alley, a closed alley. I didn't know what to do, to go right or left. For a moment it was like I lost the ability to think, my ability to reason got all clouded. I was trying to think where to run: "Well, if I go back up this street then I'll end up right where. . . ." So I ran down the street. I ran and came to a house with the windows open and the lights on. I knocked on the door a number of times, but they didn't want to answer me. Then my *compañero*, the one whose face they cut off, I remember I saw him running and screamed:

"No, wait! Let's go inside this house!" He kept running, in total desperation to get away from there, to run far away. He kept running and I didn't see him again. I told the people in the house, well, I asked if they would please let me stay there. I was begging them, saying that I wouldn't cause any problems for them, but if they would please let me in. They didn't answer me. So I jumped the fence, and then they started asking me to please leave. I said:

"Please let me just explain and then I'll go." So I told them what had happened and they asked me if anyone had seen me jump the fence. I said no.

"Are you sure?"

"Yes. No one saw me."

"No one saw you?"

"No, no one saw me."

"You're certain?"

"Yes"

"Okay. You can stay here."

And so I stayed there, alone, inside the house.

JOSÉ ARMANDO, 20, FRESHMAN. Another five *compañeros* and me hid under a Tsuru.[8] We could all see the sparks of the bullets hitting the pavement. They looked like firecrackers. And we thought: "Not again, this is the end." Our minds went blank. We said:

"Okay, well, now we're really fucked." And we saw two *compañeros* get hit and fall. We saw them lying in the street.

Then we ran about a block to an alleyway. We climbed

---

8. A Nissan car common in Mexico.

over a fence that was about three meters high and then jumped down however we could on the other side, because, you know, they were looking for us. There was a bunch of corrugated tin and other stuff on the other side of the fence. After a while, around one in the morning, it started raining. We were hiding there in the rain. There was a house there and the *tío* told us we could stay there, but not in his house: we could stay outside in the patio. A fence enclosed the patio, and we stayed there, in the rain, getting wet, until about five in the morning. We were scared, because the house was really close to where everything had happened, to where our *compañeros* were lying in the street. We hid there in the rain and we could see how the police trucks kept driving around looking for us in the streets. They stopped in front of the house a couple of times. We froze, not making a sound.

PVC, 19, FRESHMAN. Two *compañeros* went down right there. We all ran, dispersing in different directions, leaving the two *compañeros*. There was no way to go back for them without getting killed. So we all ran and splintered off in different directions. Five of us made it to an empty plot of land and hid there. We could see that cars kept passing by, cars and motorcycles, driving all around the area. About eight motorcycles went by, and trucks, lots of trucks. We stayed there. It started raining. We heard something, it sounded like screams, like someone being tortured. We heard someone screaming: "Help!" But how could we go try to help with all those people surrounding the whole area?

MIGUEL ALCOCER, 20, FRESHMAN. I saw it when they got out of their cars. They were wearing face masks. They got out and started shooting at us again. I think they first shot in the air, like giving a warning. Then they shot directly at us. Immediately, with the first shots, I had to cross the avenue toward the buses. With the first shot, I crossed and ran toward the buses. When I was just about to get to the corner, one of my *compañeros* bumped into me. I bumped into someone else, and we all fell. My legs and knees were all scraped up, and it was like I lost consciousness for a second. But then, instantly, I reacted, and got back up. When I looked back I could see the bullets ricocheting. It sounded like they were shooting us with machine guns because the shots were continuous. I think it was like three clips of rounds that they shot at us there. I got up and ran down the street. My *compañeros* ran down the street as well and I caught up with them and kept running. The gunmen were still shooting.

We had run about two blocks and could still hear the gunshots. I ran with that group of *compañeros* but, I don't know, I left them and crossed the street and ran a bit further. When I realized that I was alone, I got kind of freaked out and went back to look for the group. I saw about five students from the college coming my way.

"Where are the others?"

"I don't know," I said to them.

We kept going when we heard that some teachers from the CETEG were running our way. They were three women and they seemed really terrified and out of breath, like they couldn't run anymore. We helped them and turned down a street but realized it was a dead end. We kept going and the teachers shouted to people in the houses to open up for us, that people were trying to kill us. But none of them opened their doors for us. We went back to the street corner because the teachers said that it was dangerous to stay in that alley with nowhere to run. We were heading back to the street when we heard a bunch of trucks. We came up to the street corner and crossed over to the other corner and saw a truck with some armed men in it. The truck passed by us at full speed and maybe they didn't see us because instantly we all threw ourselves on the ground behind a car parked on the side of the road. I think that they didn't see us because they went by so fast.

When we got to the street we saw a man loading things in his house, like he had just come back from selling things, or something like that. We asked if he would let us into his house, but he didn't want to; he said no, that he didn't want any trouble. The teachers, weeping, asked him to please let us in, and so he said yes. We went inside, but only stayed for about two hours. Around three in the morning the man told us to leave his house. He said that this wasn't his problem, and that we couldn't stay there anymore. That made my *compañeros* and me feel hopeless because some *compañeros* hiding outside could see trucks driving all around looking for us, looking for any *compañeros* from the school. They told us not to leave the house because the people in those trucks could grab us. That's what made us feel so desperate about having to leave the house, because we'd been told that there were trucks all over the area looking for us. We told the teachers that the man was kicking us out of his house, and that we'd have to leave. We told them what the man had said to us. But one of the teachers lived nearby.

"Don't worry, boys," she said, "lend me your cell phone and I'll call two taxis to take me home."

She called and the first taxi came. The teacher got in. I also went in that first taxi. We went in groups of three, lying down in the back seat so that the police or gunmen wouldn't see us. We got to her house, she let us in, and then they went back to get the other *compañeros*. Then we stayed there.

COYUCO BARRIENTOS, 21, FRESHMAN. I saw a student, a junior, go down. I went back to try to help him. He was able to stand up and we kept running. There were a lot of us crammed between some parked cars. We were all mashed together. I was stuck between the wall and the edge of one of the cars and couldn't push myself further behind the car. That's when I saw where one of the individuals was shooting from the sidewalk. A number of bullets passed close to my body. Maybe they were expanding bullets because a bunch of bullet fragments hit me in the legs and hurt. At that moment I thought that I'd been hit. But I checked my legs and I didn't have any full bullet wounds. Some of the *compañeros* crammed between the cars took off running. Those of us who stayed crawled underneath the cars. Another *compañero* who was also in the marching band stayed with me under the car. And a senior from the college was lying next to me. And another *compa* from the transportation committee was there with us. There were about eight of us there. The *compa* from the marching band lying next to me was really scared. He was about to lose it.

"Calm down," I told him, "try to calm yourself down. Don't lose control, we'll find a way to get out of here."

When I started to look all around, to scan the area, I noticed that there was gasoline dripping from the car we were hiding under.

"Get the fuck out of here!," I said to all the others, "We've got to move!"

Since they were still shooting, if a bullet struck around

the gasoline we'd be screwed. I waited until the others had taken off and then ran after them. We saw an empty plot with some bathrooms toward the back of it. A fence surrounded it with some wire mesh in the corner. We went in there. I didn't see anyone coming and said: "Everyone, come quick, over here!"

Another *compa* was keeping watch. He and I were the last ones to go in. We were climbing the fence one by one while others kept a lookout. We climbed that thing however we could: some *compas* jumped, others bent down to let another use their back. When it was my turn, I don't know how, but I jumped. We were able to all get over. It was dark. We fell on top of sheets of corrugated tin. There were a bunch of metal bars and wood. It was a patio, some kind of storage area. We went as far toward the back as we could and came upon two little houses. We saw some other *compas* who had also run. They had climbed up on the roof of one of the houses. Others jumped over to the other house. They had climbed the fence and asked permission from the owners, the *tíos* that live there. And yes, they let us stay there, to hide there and wait. We started checking to see who was there, and talking about what had just happened. That was when someone told us that two students had been hit.

"One of them was *Chino*," someone told me. *Chino*, Curly, was our nickname for Dani. "It was *el Chino*."

I didn't want to believe that it was Daniel. I wanted to believe that he had been able to run and get to safety. But they started calling other *compañeros* and they also said that *Chino*, Coyuco's cousin, was dead. When we had been under the cars, Daniel's cousin had called me, asking for Daniel. He wanted to know what was happening. I told him:

"Listen, man, I can't talk right now. We're getting blown to pieces. They're shooting us, man. Let people know to come and . . . actually no, tell them not to come, tell them to wait, otherwise they'll get killed too. I can't talk. I'll call you when I can. For now we're going to try to hide." I hung up on him. That was when we ran and then went over to the houses.

We were all bunched together in that patio, trying to hide as best we could. We couldn't make any noise, to avoid being found. Any sound that we heard put us all on alert. We were just trying to figure out where we could jump and run if they came for us. Another *compa* called one of us there and told him that we need to stay put, that those assholes were still out there looking for us. We didn't hear any more gunshots, but they were still looking for us. They were driving all around the area. We waited there for more than four hours. It started raining. We tried to take cover beneath the roof of the outdoor bathrooms. The *compañeros* on the roof wouldn't come down to try and get out of the rain. They were getting soaked, and freezing cold, but they didn't want to get down. They said they'd be able to let us know if anyone was coming so that we could all run. The hours went by like that. Almost nobody had any battery power left in their cell phones. We turned them off to try and save the battery for any emergencies, to be able to make a call and let others know if something was happening.

JUAN PÉREZ, 25, FRESHMAN. I saw a *compañero* fall down. I thought they had shot him.

"A *compañero* fell down," I said, "I don't know if they hit him or not, but I saw him go down." But when I looked back he wasn't lying in the street anymore. Then, seconds later, he was right in front of me. I don't know how he did it, but he got up. He was right in front of me, with his lip all destroyed by a bullet. He was bleeding a lot. All of us standing there grabbed him and started to carry him about a block. We went about a block and knocked on the doors of two houses. We thought the building there was a Red Cross hospital. We knocked and asked for the woman there to help us, because the *compañero* was losing a lot of blood. The woman thought twice about it.

She seemed to be thinking: "Should I let them in, or no?"

She finally opened the door and we all ran in there to hide. The *compa* was bleeding badly. He was using a T-shirt to stop the blood. The nurse, well, I don't know if they were nurses, they weren't wearing uniforms. There were two women there, and a *paisa* asked them if there was a doctor on duty. They said no, that the place was closed, that it was late and there weren't any doctors there.

"Can't you call a doctor?"

The woman in charge of the clinic made a call to a cell phone, but it went straight to voice mail. At that moment the *paisa* said:

"Everyone upstairs." He was thinking that they might come shoot us again in the clinic. I asked the *paisa*:

"You want us all to go upstairs?"

"Yes," he said. So we went upstairs. The wounded *compañero* was losing it, he couldn't breathe. He typed on his cell phone:

"I can't take this anymore, I can't take it."

While we were carrying him a lot of blood fell all over the stairs, everywhere, splashing all over everything. Upstairs he sat at a table: the table was covered in blood. We thought he'd faint. We took him back downstairs. A *compa* went back out into the street to look for a taxi, but the drivers didn't want to help. The taxis were driving around like they were there to keep watch over us. The same taxi drove by again, and once again the *compas* pleaded:

"Help us take our *compañero*; some people hurt us."

But no, the taxi driver didn't care. The *compañero* couldn't stand it anymore. We went back upstairs. When I stuck my head out of the upstairs window, the soldiers' truck was there. I don't know how they got inside, but they started cocking their guns and everyone went downstairs.

The soliders ordered us to go downstairs.

I hid. There were three of us hiding up there. But then a *compa* went back and said: "Ok, fuck it, let them just take us already." So we all went downstairs. I had a backpack with me. I always carry some cookies and water in case I get hungry.

"You all with the backpacks," the soliders said, "drop them." We set them down.

"If you have a cell phone, put it on the table." We all took out our cell phones and put them on the table. Before putting mine on the table I took out the chip and hid it.

The commander, I think, came in and asked us: "Where are you all from?"

"We're from Ayotzinapa." We thought that they were going to help us, that they would support us. They didn't.

"Alright, everyone sit over there." We all sat down where they told us. They asked the *compa* who had been shot in the lip for his name and where he's from.

A *paisa* said to the soldiers: "Please, help us! The *compa* is bleeding to death! Call an ambulance!" But the commander didn't pay him the least attention.

"What you all are doing is wrong," the commander started saying to us. He said that we needed to show our parents that we are really students by making good grades. Then he said that an ambulance would be there in half an hour. Then they walked outside and left. Just like that, like nothing was happening.

A doctor showed up and told us he was going to close

and lock up the clinic and ordered us to get out. I thought at some point he would help us, but he never did. He didn't help the *compa* with the bullet wound. He could have given him a piece of cotton with alcohol, but he didn't. Nothing.

We all went outside and ran, scared. We thought that the men with guns would come back again since the soldiers didn't help us or guard us. The solidiers didn't support us at all. They left us there like nothing had happened, and we took off running.

OMAR GARCÍA, 24, SOPHOMORE. We went to the Cristina Clinic and took shelter there until the soldiers arrived. They busted in together with the owner of the clinic. He was with them; they brought him in their patrol trucks. And, well, the shit hit the fan there in a big way, because of the serious lack of support from the army. They could see we had a wounded person with us. We identified ourselves as students from Ayotzinapa, and said there was a teacher with us. They had to have helped us, without a doubt. They realized we weren't criminals, that we were students, that there was a seriously wounded person with us. They should have done whatever they could to help him. And they could have done a great deal: they had trucks they could have used to take him to the hospital immediately. We didn't care if they came in threatening us and saying we were criminals, we wanted them to help our *compañero*. If they were going to arrest us, put us on trial, or whatever, well that all comes later: the first thing is to help the wounded. But they didn't do that. Instead, they made note of our information, they took our photographs, and they left threatening us saying that the municipal police were on their way. What's more, when they asked for our information they said, crystal clear, even repeating it, pointing at us all:

"Give us your real names; if you give us false names, you'll never be found."

At that moment we didn't know what was happening. We thought that we'd be able to go to the jail to look for the *compañeros* who had been taken, that we'd pay their bail or whatever and get them out. We thought that there'd be some kind of a trial or legal process and we'd get them out like we had before, in earlier years, because we're students, and we always get out of jail with political pressure or whatever. We didn't know they were orchestrating a forced disappearance.

EDGAR YAIR, 18, FRESHMAN. I ran straight ahead. When I had made it about a half a block I heard someone shout that a *compañero* was wounded, for us to wait. We stopped to see what was happening. And we saw a *compa* who'd been wounded in the mouth; he didn't have a top lip anymore, he didn't have anything there. We carried him.

"Bring him here inside our house," some neighbors said to us.

But we didn't want to, we wanted to find a hospital. We shouted out to them asking where we could find a hospital. They said we could find one a bit farther down the street. So we ran.

There was a hospital there. We knocked on the door, but it was an X-ray laboratory and two women came out. I don't know if they were nurses or if they were just caretakers there. But they told us that they couldn't help us because the doctor wasn't there. They said that they didn't have the materials to operate because the place was just an X-ray lab.

But they said we could stay there until daybreak. And we said okay. We tried to stop a taxi, but none of them wanted to help us take the wounded *compa* to the hospital. We were there in that building for about an hour when the soldiers arrived.

The *compañero* was pretty much bleeding to death. He took out his cell phone and wrote on the screen for us to get him out of there, that he couldn't take it anymore, that he was dying. And we tried everything to get him out of there, but the soldiers showed up. It seemed like they were going to arrest us. They took all our phones away. They took our pictures. Their commander told us that we had no business being there, and that we were looking to get killed. And we started telling him that we were students from the college here. But he said no, that for him we were criminals, and we'd have to prove we were students by making good grades.

There was also a teacher there helping us and he asked the soldiers to help us, to take our wounded *compa* to get help. The doctor came at the end. I think the two women called him. He arrived, but the soldiers were there and wouldn't let him help the wounded *compa*. The doctor said he was the owner of the place and that was it. He didn't say anything else. The military commander told us we couldn't stay there, that we'd have to find someplace else, but not there.

IVÁN CISNEROS, 19, SOPHOMORE. I didn't run very far because I saw some people carrying a *compañero*, the junior who got shot in the mouth. We helped carry that *compa* and took him to where there was a clinic. We walked a block or two blocks at most and found a clinic. There were some nurses there, but they said that no doctors were there. I think the nurses took off and left us there. We told the boys to go upstairs and not come back down. The wall downstairs was glass, with all the windows, and you could see inside. We were scared that they'd see us. We were there for a while. The *compañero* who was bleeding half to death took out his cell phone and wrote:

"Get me out of here; I'm dying."

I went upstairs to check on the *compañeros* and when I came down, some ten minutes later, I saw that the soldiers were outside at the door.

"Hey, man," we said to *La Parca*, "the soldiers are outside." We thought they were going to help us, and we opened the door. They came inside with the characteristic subtlety of the military.

"Okay, assholes, everyone downstairs!"

They pointed their guns at us and herded us all to one part of the waiting room. Then they told us something like this:

"If you've all got the balls to start a shitstorm, then have the balls to face the consequences."

They made everyone come downstairs. They made us put all our belongings—cell phones, keys—on the table there in the waiting room. And basically they told us we'd all be arrested by the police for being on private property, for breaking and entering, or something like that. They said they were going to hand us over to the municipal police. And then we all said no, that the police had been shooting at us earlier.

"You all are the ones who invaded this place," they said. And then they told us that two of our *compañeros* were dead in the street. And we didn't know. It hit us like a bucket of cold water.

They took our photos there and then pretty much sent us running. One person stayed behind with the wounded *compa* to wait for an ambulance, and the rest of us ran about a block and then turned left. A *tía* took us in there.

JUAN SALGADO, FRESHMAN. I kept running and about two blocks down the street I saw some people carrying a *compa* who was bleeding. I thought: "Damn, what happened to this *compa*?" I stopped to see what had happened. That was when I saw that his lips were gone. The *compañeros* were getting tired and I went to take over for one of them. The shots were still ringing out and we kept going as best we could. We were running and asking if there was hospital or clinic nearby. And a woman, a pregnant woman from the second story of a house shouted out to us that there was a clinic.

"Where? Where?"

"There, right where you are, in front of you, that's it."

"Thank you!"

We knocked and there were two receptionists there. The lights were all off, but the receptionists were there.

"Please, open up!" But, it's like they were thinking twice about opening up for us or not. "Please, open up! A *compañero* is wounded! Please!"

Pretty much in tears we were asking them to help us. When they opened the door we all ran inside; there were about twenty-seven of us. The others had run as best they could. A bunch of us hid beneath the stairs, sitting down there. The wounded *compa* sat down on a sofa, bleeding.

"A doctor," I said, "a surgeon for the *compañero*."

"He's not here right now, the doctor's not here; I'll have to call him."

One of the receptionists kept calling until the doctor answered. He said that he wasn't going to go to the clinic because it was too late.

"Please, at least call a taxi or an ambulance so we can take him to the hospital."

The receptionists could see that the *compañero* was seriously wounded. But the only thing they said was that the doctor couldn't help because it was nighttime, that they couldn't help us. That's what they said, but we saw them call a taxi. The taxi service wouldn't send a driver to pick us up. They weren't going to put their drivers at risk while there was shooting nearby. The receptionists didn't want to call an ambulance.

We were there for about thirty or forty minutes when the soldiers came. Two military trucks arrived and they gathered us all in the waiting room and made us show them all the things we had with us. They went through our stuff like we were the suspects or something. They took note of how many of us were there. That's when I noticed something strange: when the soldiers arrived the receptionists were gone. The soldiers looked through the clinic, but the receptionists were gone; we were the only ones there. I asked myself: "What is this, what is going on here, how is it that the receptionists are gone and the soldiers are taking notes about all of us? Why aren't they helping the *compa* who is seriously wounded?"

"At least call an ambulance or a taxi to take him to the hospital," I said.

But they didn't want to call an ambulance or a taxi. The soldiers said they couldn't arrest us because that's not their job. They said their job was to patrol and watch over things, but that it was the job of the municipal police to arrest us. But they said they would be keeping watch out in the street because there were three bodies lying on the pavement. That's when we learned. We were asking ourselves: Whose bodies? Were they *compañeros* from the school?

The soldier in charge said that he was going to call the police to come get us because we were committing acts of vandalism. He said that he understood that we had to struggle, but that it would be better if we were to show our struggle by bettering ourselves academically and making good grades. He was saying that what we do is bad and that it would be better if we just learned to make do with what we're given; that if we'd get a job we would be lucky, and if not, then tough. That's pretty much what we took away from what he said, that we should give up our struggle because it only led to wounded *compañeros*. That was the lecture he gave us. And that's how they qualified our struggle: vandalism. And he said he was going to call the municipal police so they would come, arrest us, and take us to the local jail, Barandillas.

We told him no, that we didn't trust the municipal police, that if they were going to arrest us, they should do it themselves.

"That's not our job," they kept insisting. "If we get mixed up in this then they'll come after us, and that might not go so well for us." That's what the soldier said. And so we asked him to call an ambulance for the *compañero*.

"The ambulance is on its way," he said. "We're going to leave, you can wait here for the ambulance that will take your *compañero*."

We said to ourselves: "No, now they all know where we are." But we also didn't want to leave the *compa* with the wounded lips.

"Leave me with him, if the ambulance comes we'll wait for it and I'll go with him to the hospital, you all go, run, hide wherever you can," one *compañero* said when the soldiers had left.

There was a teacher with us too. I don't remember

where he taught, but he stayed with us and helped us, and he also stayed with the wounded *compa*. An overweight doctor showed up. The only thing he said was that we needed to take the *compa* to a hospital, nothing else. And so we took off running wherever we could.

PEDRO CRUZ MENDOZA, IGUALA-BASED TEACH-ER, MEMBER OF THE STATE COORDINATION OF EDUCATION WORKERS OF GUERRERO (CETEG). Everyone ran in different directions; we all lost track of each other, hiding wherever we could. I ran down Álvarez and threw myself in one of the buses. I hid on the floor there for a while. I said to the boys: "Don't stand up!" The shooting lasted, I'd guess, about three to five minutes. I was down inside the bus for a good while and said to the *compañeros* from Ayotzi: "Don't stand up, don't stand up, hold on, hold on, don't stand up," because the gunmen were still shooting. I thought that if we stood up they'd be able to target us. When there was a break in the shooting I took out my phone and called a *compañero* in Tixtla. I put my cell on speakerphone.

"Hey, Juan, they are shooting at us!"

"Hide! Take cover," he said.

"Send the press!"

He was the statewide spokesperson for the CETEG, so a number of reporters know and get along well with him.

"Give me your phone, prof," a boy from Ayotzi said to me, "I'll film what's going on."

"No, no, no, no, no, if you go out there to film they'll kill you; no, let's get out of here, let's go."

We went about fifteen or twenty meters from the bus where we'd been hiding and saw a guy who was bleeding badly. We went up to him and grabbed him, and one of the boys asked me:

"Where should we go now, to the general hospital?"

"No," I said, "it is really far from here to the general hospital, it is very far." It was about five kilometers. "We'll never make it walking there; he'll die on us."

We went back to Álvarez from the little street we had turned onto and tried to stop a number of taxis, but no one would stop for us. They threw their cars in reverse and took off. Then I remembered.

"There is a clinic near here," I said. "Let's go to the clinic, there's one close by." And I remembered the Cristina Clinic.

We arrived and there were only two nurses there. The clinic was closed but there were two nurses. We knocked loudly on the door. The nurses came to the door, but they didn't want to open up for us.

"Please, *tía*," the boys begged, "let us in."

"Listen, this boy is dying," I added, "please let us in, he's dying."

And we held the *compañero* up to the door window so they could see him. Only then did they feel some compassion and open the door. We all went inside. But they left. They left us alone there. There was no doctor on duty. So we sat the *compañero* down in the little waiting room. We sat him down and started fanning him with whatever we could: our hands, a T-shirt, someone found a magazine there and used that to fan his mouth saying that he might choke on his blood. It is a lie that he was able to talk. He took out his cell phone and wrote:

"I need air, I'm dying, I feel really bad."

He had to use his cell phone to communicate with us. Seeing how bad he was I started to call *compañeros* from the CETEG to come and help us because this kid was dying. I even called one of my brothers to tell him that we'd been shot at. I thought they were going to kill me, for real, that they'd kill all of us. I called my brother and told him what had happened.

"If they kill me," I said, "don't let them accuse me of being involved in organized crime; they killed us, they're going to kill us, because of what happened tonight." My brother knew what was going on and called back later to see how I was doing.

So I kept trying, with *compañeros* from the CETEG. First, a *compañera* called a taxi for us. I went outside. It was drizzling. I told the taxi driver:

"Hey, there's a wounded guy in here, he's dying."

"No, I can't give you all a ride," he said. "We received instructions not to give rides to any of the wounded." The taxi driver! Just then another taxi pulled up next to him.

"Hey, they're asking me to pick up a wounded person," he said.

"No, you can't pick him up," the second driver said.

"Come on, man," I said, angry, "we're human beings, some day you'll need our help." But he left.

I called my *compañeros* again: "Listen, please help us, he's dying, this kid is dying." I called one *compañero* who has a small truck. I called him and said: "Come pick us up, this kid is dying on us."

"We're on our way," he said. "Where are you?"

I told him that we were inside the Cristina Clinic. As they were getting close, the *compañero* called me and said:

"We're here, but we can't pick you up. The army is on their way. We're just going to drive by." And they drove by the clinic. When my *compañero* told me this I saw the army trucks park right in front of the clinic. The wall has like some smoked glass, but since we had all the lights inside the hospital turned off, we could easily see out in the street. Two army trucks with between twelve and fifteen soldiers pulled up. I told the Ayotzinapa students:

"Run! Run! The army is coming!" Since I had read in *Proceso* about the Tlatlaya case,[9] the first thing I thought was: "These fuckers are going to blow us to pieces." And I said to the boys: "Run, run!" We all ran.

The *compas* grabbed the wounded guy and carried him upstairs. Since everyone had run upstairs and the clinic has a long hallway, I ran down to the end of the hallway and went into a bathroom on the left-hand side. I didn't have anything at all to protect myself with. I bent down and thought: "Well, fuck it, I'll wait for the gunshots here." Then I heard the soldiers' insults.

"Okay, everyone downstairs," said the soldiers, "sons of who-knows-what, everyone downstairs!"

I thought: "They're going to kill us all here, I just hope they kill me with everyone else, because if they kill me back here no one will find me." I left the bathroom. The soldiers saw me and shouted:

"Hands in the air! Hands in the air!"

I raised my hands and walked toward them with my hands in the air. They had all the boys gathered there in the little waiting room. Others were still coming downstairs.

"Lift up your shirts!"

We lifted up our shirts, but they didn't stop aiming their guns at us.

"I want all your cell phones and wallets on the table!"

And we took out our cell phones and wallets and took them over to the table.

---

9. Pedro Cruz Mendoza refers here to one of the first articles citing eyewitness testimony to an army massacre of 22 civilians in Tlatlaya, State of Mexico, on June 30, 2014. Pablo Ferri Tórtola, "Veintiuno de los 'delincuentes' abatidos en Tlatlaya fueron 'fusilados' por el Ejército," *Proceso*, September 17, 2014.

"I want your complete and real names, otherwise they'll never find you. Do you have ID cards?" Some said that they didn't have theirs and I said:

"I have my ID."

"Who are you?"

"I'm a teacher."

"And this is what you teach?"

"No, no, no, no. Listen, sir, I came to help them because they were attacked, they were hurt. We're here together but I didn't teach them any of this."

"Alright, take down all their names, names!"

Some of the phones started ringing and the soldiers said: "Answer, answer; put the phones on speakerphone!" They let us answer our phones, but using speakerphone. My *compañero* from Tixtla called me, the one I had told that they were shooting at us, but I wasn't able to answer. The commander in charge said to us:

"There are two guys dead in the street out there and my guess is that they're two of yours. But you all have busted into a private hospital, it's called breaking and entering, we're going to call the municipal police so they can arrest you all." And there I had to say something because the truth is, we were scared, all the boys were scared, but because I'm older and from Iguala, I felt a moral obligation to speak out. I said:

"Listen, sir, the municipal police will kill us, they'll turn us over to . . . they were the ones shooting at us."

"What do you mean, it was them?"

"Yes," and the students started speaking up: "Yes sir, it was them!"

"Okay then, we're going to investigate, we'll ask around."

And the commander stepped outside with his bodyguards, but left us inside with soldiers aiming at us. They never stopped aiming at us; they never lowered their guns. And there we were with our shirts pulled up and our hands in the air. We stayed like that the whole time. They came back in and I said:

"Excuse me, sir, we need an ambulance, this boy is dying."

"It's on its way," he said. "I called one, it'll be right here!" He said it like that, in an insulting, commanding tone. "Everyone come over here!" He called the boys over to the hallway and bunched them all together, leaving me alone; they didn't call me over. They were all bunched together in the hall but only about two meters away from me. I could hear everything they were saying.

Some of the boys squatted down, others were sitting down and the commander started to lecture them:

"This is why you come here? This is why you ask your parents to give you money? This is why you are studying, to do things like this? This is what they teach you at that school? No, no, boys; think about it." And then he gave them a litany of advice. The guy with the gunshot wound was asking for oxygen, and the soldiers screamed:

"Sit him down! Sit him down!"

"He's dying on us; he wants to breathe, we can't sit him down," we said.

When I saw that the soldiers were leaving, I said a second time: "Excuse me, sir, we need an ambulance, this boy is dying."

"I already called! It's on the way! Alright, you all can stay here, the area is now under the army's control, there won't be any problems."

"Sir," I asked for the third time, "and the ambulance?"

"DON'T YOU UNDERSTAND THAT I ALREADY CALLED FOR IT! You all can stay here, nothing is going to happen." And they went; they left us there. I told the students:

"Boys, don't go, there are a bunch of houses of teachers from the CETEG, I'm from the CETEG, don't be afraid, we can help to hide you all." But one of them said:

"Let's get the fuck out of here; they're going to kill us here." They were very scared.

One of them, I think whoever was in charge, said to me: "Prof, will you stay with the wounded guy?" There was no way I'd say no.

"Sure, don't worry," I said.

"Let's go, now," someone else said, "they're going to come back, they'll come back; let's hide under a bridge, let's go." And they all took off running. That's when Omar came back. He ran about halfway down the street and then came back and said:

"Prof, I'll stay with you." Another one came back and said:

"I'll stay too."

"No," Omar said, "you're not staying, you're going, go with them." So Omar and I stayed with the wounded guy. That was when I met Omar. I went back to call my *compañeros*. That was when Doctor Herrera arrived. The door wasn't closed and he came inside. I introduced myself:

"Doctor, look, I'm a teacher, they attacked us, this boy is wounded."

"Yeah, yeah, I already know what happened. There are two young men dead out there in the street and no one has come for them."

"Don't tell me that, Doctor, really?"

"Yeah, I just came from over there and no one is taking them away, there they are, dead in the street."

"Look, as you can see, this boy is wounded, no one

wants to give us a ride, would you be able to take us to the hospital?"

"Damn, kid, they hit you good, you'll need surgery. Yeah, I'll help you."

But all that he cared about was walking through his clinic and making sure nothing had been stolen. The doctor even said: "Listen, teacher, you all came right to organized crime's front door, those dudes live right there, they are from Teloloapan, I know them." He was referring to a mafia gang called *Los Peques*, The Little Ones, because they live around there. I remember that perfectly.

Since the doctor wasn't helping us, I called my *compañeros* again, but right then a taxi pulled up in front of the clinic. I told the taxi driver: "Hey, there's a boy whose been hurt, could you give us a ride?"

"Sure, sure, get in," he said.

When the doctor came back out we were getting in the taxi. He, in all honesty, didn't help us in any way, not even to help get the wounded boy inside the cab. Before the taxi came I asked him nicely: "Doctor, could you help us? Because no one wants to pick us up, no taxis." He said yes, but then went about surveying his clinic. I told both of the students:

"Don't say anything, nothing at all." I told Omar: "Get in the back with him, don't say anything, I'll talk to the driver." It was still drizzling. We had put a shirt up to Edgar's face to . . . I don't know . . . to slow the bleeding.

"What happened? Are there a bunch of patients there?"

"Yes, the hospital is full. I think they've got several surgeries scheduled. Can you believe it? Please, if you don't mind, would you take us to the hospital?"

"Yes, sure, of course. What happened to your *compañero*?"

"We got into a fight at a bar and they hit him with a bottle in the mouth. Can you believe it?"

"Damn, that sucks. Did you all hear about the shooting?"

"No, no, in the bar you can't hear anything with all that noise, we didn't hear anything. Really, there was a shooting?"

"Yeah, there was a shooting around here, that's what we were told."

"No, we had no idea."

And so we talked on the drive about insecurity and all that. When we arrived I stayed with the taxi. Omar took Edgar inside and stayed with him.

EDGAR ANDRÉS VARGAS, 20, JUNIOR. I started going around; I took some photos. Some guys were placing rocks around the bullet shells. There was blood in the bus, by the door, and by the entrance. I took photos of all that. I went to look for a friend from my hometown who had gone on the action. I don't know what time it was when I found him. That guy is from my town. I asked him how he was. The guy was scared, for real. I asked about the others and he said:

"The cops took them; they took them away."

I talked to him for a while and then went to look around some more. I ran into a guy from my study group and asked him:

"And your brother?" He told me that he couldn't find his brother, that he wasn't there. I said:

"Maybe he's with the other guys that the police took."

He said maybe so. In that moment we never even thought about our *compas* being disappeared. I thought it would be like always: the police take you, they hold you for a while, ask you questions, and then they let you go. But no.

After a bit my girlfriend called me and asked me where I was. I told her:

"I'm here where everything went down. I'm here."

She asked me if it was still a good idea for her to visit me at the school. Since I didn't know about the disappearance, I thought that it wouldn't go on much longer, that it wasn't going to be such a problem. So I told her:

"No, don't worry, come."

She said okay and told me she'd get in around five, five in the morning. After that I went to talk to the guy from my hometown and he was telling me about everything that had happened. Three of us were standing there together. There were others nearby and all around. Everything was calm, when out of nowhere we heard gunshots.

I don't know what I did in that moment. I was the last person of the three standing there. I don't know where the guy from my hometown went, I lost sight of him instantly. I lost track of everyone and threw myself down on the ground. Honestly, I don't know when exactly the bullet hit me; I didn't feel it. But the gunshots were sounding when I heard a whizzing sound in this ear, a whizzing sound. I was already down on the ground at that point. I went to the ground and in that moment heard the whizzing sound and started to see blood falling. I think that when I heard the whizzing sound is when they hit me. I lost all of this part, what they call the upper maxillary. I didn't know what to do in that moment and I stayed there in the middle of the street. I stayed lying down with my hands up by my face. I saw the bullets hitting the pavement. The machine-gun bursts didn't stop. Bullets were hitting near my body. I lifted my head and looked back. I didn't see anyone there and looked to my right side and the only thing I could see were something like sparks from where the shots were coming.

And I stayed there, I don't know, like I was paralyzed for a moment. And when I saw the blood I couldn't believe it.

"No," I said to myself. I couldn't believe they had hit me. At that moment I started crawling. When I arrived at the first bus, the first of the three buses, I stayed there for about five minutes.

I didn't see anyone in those five minutes.

When the shooting paused, there were moments when the shots paused, I saw when some people—and I don't know from where they came—started running. I was there up against the bus. I don't think anyone saw me. I had my hand like this trying to. . . . I saw the blood that fell all over my hand and I couldn't believe it, I couldn't believe that they had shot me. I thought: "No, no, no." I looked back to where I was before, to where I had been standing before and I was able to see the guys, the ones who were killed. One of them I think was already dead because there was a pool of blood around him. The other one was screaming. I started walking away, but the shooting went on and on.

I kept walking. A bit farther ahead, near the second bus, I ran into Omar, I think. No, it wasn't him. It was another *compañero* who was with several others, but he was the only one who saw me. He shouted out to his *compas* to wait because he had seen me. My nickname at the school is *el Oaxaco*, the Oaxacan, so he shouted:

"*Oaxaco* is hurt, we've got to help him!" Something like that. They all came back and tried to carry me. Well, they did carry me for a bit. The shooting had stopped.

I saw a woman open her front door and shout to us: "Bring him in here, hide in here!" She shouted something like that.

"No," the guys shouted back, "he's wounded, we're going to take him to a clinic near here!"

They had already seen the clinic. At that moment I told them to let me down, that I could walk, and I did walk. We went up to the clinic's door. I think it was a nurse, or someone in charge of the place who came to the door. They asked her if the doctor was there and she said no, that the doctor wasn't there, that no one was there. We asked her, well, they asked her—more guys had arrived—to let us hide there. And so we all went inside the clinic. The nurse didn't want to let us in at first, but then we all went inside and then I think the nurses left. I don't know what they went to do, but I didn't see them anymore. And there we were, freshmen, sophomores, and juniors. In fact, the student secretary was there, and so were a number of students from my group.

I sat down on the couch. I don't remember if it was Omar, I don't remember at what point Omar came up to me, but first I sat down in a chair, there were several chairs there, and had my head bowed. A number of *compañeros* came up to me and told me to hold on. And there was a teacher there. I'd seen that teacher before. I recognized his face because I'd seen him in a march in December, I recognized him. I didn't know who he was or anything, but his face was really familiar to me. Then the secretary, I think, told us to go upstairs; the clinic had two or three stories. We went upstairs. I couldn't speak. I wrote using my cell phone to *Parca*, the secretary and a *compañero* of mine, telling him to find a way to get me out of there, to take me to a hospital because the bleeding wouldn't stop. Then I sat down at a desk in a hallway and stayed there for a while. I told the guys up there, well, I wrote to them in my cell phone, to find a way to get me out of there. I don't know how much time I was there, to be honest, it was like I lost all notion of time. So many things came into my head: mainly my family, my mom, my dad, they came to mind and I thought about how,

when my mom found out about this, well, she would cry. I
didn't want to tell her.

I don't know how they contacted the clinic's doctor and
asked him to come. One guy told me to hold on, that the
doctor was on the way. But before that, a nurse had told me
that they couldn't help me because the doctor wasn't there.
I think she was the one who called him. And the doctor arrived and said:

"This is serious, we can't help him here, we don't have
the tools." And that was the only thing he said. I didn't see
where he went after that.

I think I then went back upstairs, but the thing is that
when the soldiers arrived a bunch of us were upstairs. We
were hiding when the soldiers came in and told us all to
come down. I didn't go downstairs and stayed on the second
floor a little while. The students told the soldiers that someone was wounded.

"Make him come downstairs too," said the soldier.
They told me to come downstairs and I did. So at some
point I told my parents. I don't know if it was before the
soldiers came or after. I can't remember. I think it was afterward because they came, they told me to come downstairs,
I did, and there were I don't know how many soliders there.
They were like six, seven, eight, and there were more of
them outside. Those idiots said a shitload of stuff like:

"You all thought you were tough guys, so take it, you
came looking for it." They asked for our names. One guy
said his name and then a soldier said:

"Tell us your real names, your true names and ages."
And so everyone started saying their names, and I think the
soldiers were taking notes.

They told the soldiers my name. I was sitting on a couch
and Omar was next to me. He was telling me to hold on and

he said, I'm not sure he's the one who asked the soldiers to take me to the hospital. They took pictures of me, and pictures of the place. They told us all to put our cell phones on the table. I think one guy's phone rang. He asked for permission to answer it and they said no, they told him not to answer. The phones all stayed there on the table. They started taking pictures, and one soldier said that there were two guys lying dead outside. I didn't really pay a lot of attention to what the soldiers were saying. I think they left after that. They said they'd called the hospital, asking them to send an ambulance that never arrived. The teacher was there. In fact, the soldiers asked the teacher what he was doing there, what he was doing with the students, what his job was. He said he was a teacher and that he had come to help after the police had attacked the students. Something like that. The soldiers didn't arrest anyone there.

At some point I asked Omar to call my parents to let them know. I found their number and then he called them. He said that there was a problem, that I was hurt. Omar told them that I was wounded, that I'd been hit by a bullet. My dad asked where I'd been shot and Omar said in the face, near the mouth. My dad at that moment thought that it was this part of my face, the lower jaw. The only thing my dad said to Omar was for him to please stay with me, not to leave me alone. Then he asked to speak to me. Omar told him that I couldn't speak. Then he just held the phone between us. My dad said, crying I think, for me to hold on, to hold on a bit, and that he was on his way. And I heard my mom's voice. When my dad said "my son" into the phone, my mom quickly got out of bed and screamed, asking what had happened to me. My dad didn't tell me right then, but my mom—I don't know, I guess it is a mother's instinct—my mom screamed, almost in tears. I heard that through the phone. My dad was telling me to hold on, that he was on his way, telling me not to give up, to have faith in God, because we are, we belong to a religion.

"I'm going to pray for you right now," my dad said—no, wait, he didn't say that. He said: "Your mom is going to pray for you," or something like that, I can't remember. When I heard my mom's voice I felt really bad. I felt sad, in all honesty. I wrote a message in my phone. I told my dad to pray for me, to not leave me alone, to take care of my mom, and to tell her that I was going to be okay. I sent that message.

We realized that the ambulance wasn't coming. The teacher was trying to find a way to get me to the hospital. He had called a number of taxis, but no one was available to pick me up. There we were just waiting. I don't know what time it was. They said that I was there for about two hours bleeding out. I didn't notice the time, but I do remember that I left a lot of blood there. I was sitting down and started feeling my body weaken. I got so tired. I wanted badly to go to sleep. I really couldn't take the tiredness. I started to close my eyes for little bits. Omar would wake me up:

"Hold on, hold on." He said that the taxi was on its way. I lifted my head and everything seemed blurry and I got really hot. I wanted to take off my jacket, but when I took it off—I did take it off—but when I took it off I started getting cold and I put it back on again and then I felt hot. I felt like I was choking, like I couldn't get enough air. Then I started to feel really bad and my face started to hurt. It hadn't hurt me earlier, it just felt hot. After the soldiers had arrived it started hurting and I felt my head like it was heavy. It started hurting and then the pain was getting more and more intense. I don't know what time it was. Then a taxi arrived. The teacher and Omar got in. I think the taxi driver asked: "What happened to him?" or something like that. The teacher said that we had been in a cantina drinking and someone had hit me in the face with a bottle. I grabbed a towel that was there in the taxi and put it under my mouth to try and not stain the car. I felt like my body was shutting down. I felt tired, really sleepy. I could feel my body trembling.

By the time we arrived at the hospital my vision was all blurry. It was already drizzling. When it started raining I felt cold, really cold. I got to the emergency room. I remember that there were a lot of people there in the emergency room but when a nurse saw me she instantly called a doctor. They sat me on a stretcher. It all happened really fast. They were stitching up my hand—it was cut open—while they started taking off my clothes, all of my clothes. They asked me what had happened. I didn't answer. In fact, when they were stitching up my hand I already had my eyes closed and I couldn't hear them very well. Everything sounded distorted, all the voices. They told me to lie down. In the instant that I lay down I went to sleep. From that moment on I lost consciousness, I slept.

My mom says I woke up four days later.

NOTES FROM MY NOTEBOOK OF AN INTERVIEW, CONDUCTED TOGETHER WITH MARCELA TURATI, WITH DOCTOR RICARDO HERRERA, SURGEON AND DIRECTOR OF THE CRISTINA PRIVATE HOSPITAL, IGUALA, GUERRERO, 10 OCTOBER 2014.
Herrera: They took the place over by force. It was all covered in blood. I called the police, but the army came. I didn't call the army. And when I asked the soldier why the police didn't come, he told me that the police had orders not to leave their stations.

Turati: Did you attend to the wounded?

Herrera: No.

Turati: Why not?

Herrera: It wasn't my obligation. If someone arrives nicely, then I attend to him or her. But if people come all aggressive, hitting the place. . . . I called the police, but the army came. The soldiers called an ambulance. But they took the wounded guy off in a taxi. He did not have any gunshot wounds. A bullet grazed his lips. He was walking around and talking like normal.

Turati: He almost died.

Herrera: Of fright, I guess. But he was mixed up in adult things. And that's what's going to happen to all those *ayotzinapos.*

Turati: I hope not.

Herrera: I hope so. Because that school is worthless. They invade property. That is a crime. They leave everything dirty, ugly, and the government has to pay for it, and that bothers me because it drains the government. They are criminals.

Gibler: That is a crime? That seems wrong to you? So, cutting off their faces, taking out their eyes, cutting off their limbs, and incinerating their bodies: that seems right to you?

Herrera: Yes. Truthfully: yes.

SERGIO OCAMPO, 58, JOURNALIST WITH THE AUTONOMOUS UNIVERSITY OF GUERRERO RADIO STATION AND CHILPANCINGO-BASED STAFF WRITER FOR *LA JORNADA*. The guys from FUNE, the

United Front of Teachers College Alumni, called a press conference at eleven-thirty. We arrived where they had set up a protest camp and they told us that one of the students had been killed. The events had just taken place, and the first person killed that they spoke of was the student who is now in a coma. He didn't die. With a number of colleagues we decided to go to Iguala. We were going to go on our own. When the teachers heard we were going they said:

"Hey, let's go."

We decided together with the teachers and the students there, and the other reporters, to all go to Iguala in a caravan. We felt a bit braver since we would be about thirty people. We left in two cars and one bus. I was driving one of the cars. On the road a reporter from another newspaper told me:

"Hey, my editor tells me it's not safe to go to Iguala."

"Well," I said, "precisely because it is not safe to go to Iguala, we need to go and find out what's happening!" And then we came to Santa Teresa and saw the soccer team's bus, the Chilpancingo Avispones. The bus was completely destroyed. I saw a referee whom I know.

"I came to look for my son," he told me. "They called me saying they had all been shot."

"And you came alone?"

"Yes, I'm here alone."

"That's brave. We came in a caravan."

There was one federal police car there, but otherwise they were completely alone.

We got to Iguala around one-thirty in the morning. As soon as we got near the city, the narco lookouts, the *halcones*, started following us. The municipal police were out as well. We got stopped at a municipal police checkpoint. A police officer asked me:

"Where are you going?"

"Officer, we heard that something was happening in Iguala."

"No, nothing's happening here."

"Really? Come on, where's the trouble?"

"Take the boulevard. And who are they?"

"Students."

We were there at the checkpoint for about twenty minutes, a while. The energy was tense there. Knowing how they operate in total impunity, surely those dudes were there. They covered all the tasks: they were police, they were traffic cops, they were hit men. Or, they are. When we got to the corner of Álvarez and Periférico an army captain began questioning us.

"What are you all doing here?"

"We are reporters."

"And them?"

"They're teachers and students. They came to look for their friends."

When we got there the two boys were lying in the street. No one had even covered them. Right there, well, the boys who came with us starting crying.

LENIN OCAMPO, 33, STAFF PHOTOGRAPHER WITH *EL SUR* IN CHILPANCINGO. I host a radio program every Friday. It starts at ten at night and goes until one in the morning. On Friday the twenty-sixth, people started posting on social media that there had been a confrontation with the boys from Ayotzi. And a number of guys who graduated from Ayotzi and listen to my radio program started calling me, saying: "Hey, they killed two students," or, "They killed a student."

Around eleven that night a guy who was there where

it was all happening called me. So the student, on the air, started asking for help, saying that they were alone and they had been attacked. That's what he said. He said one person was dead and they had taken a number of *compañeros* and that they were afraid and asking for security from the state government. About twenty minutes after he called in to the radio, they were strafed with machine-gun fire. That was when they killed two students. And there was a group of reporters there, too. They were in a press conference when an armed group shot at them all. The Iguala-based reporters also got shot at. My editors at the newspaper called me and said:

"What's the chance that you all could go?"

"I don't know," I said, "who is going?"

But we put together a caravan of reporters, eight of us in two trucks. We made plans to meet up at a location on the outskirts of Chilpancingo and head out at around half past midnight. In that lapse of time we also waited for a bus from the school to go in caravan with them as well.

As we were arriving in Zumpango, which is about ten minutes from Chilpancingo, we got a text message from a *compañera* who was at the press conference telling us that they had just been shot at. After that text we didn't hear anything more. When we were a bit beyond Zumpango we got another text from the crime beat reporters in Iguala telling us that the Avispones had been attacked. The Avispones are a soccer team from Chilpancingo. The reporters told us that three people had been killed in that attack. We were driving on the highway; there was no police presence. We came to Santa Teresa, the place where the Avispones bus was stopped. The bus had been traveling from Iguala to Chilpancingo and was left half turned over in a ditch. It had a ton of bullet holes all over it; I'd guess about three hundred. There were still some of the soccer players' parents there, including a referee who was all worried because they couldn't find some of the players. Right there they also attacked a taxi and killed a woman.

So when we got to Iguala, there was a police checkpoint. It looked like they were waiting for battle. The municipal police were all spread out across the highway. Like they were in battle position. We pulled up and the *compañero* who was driving rolled down the window. The police officer said:

"Get out."

"No. We're not getting out. We're reporters."

"No? We don't give a fuck what you are, get out."

"We're not getting out."

We didn't get out of the truck, but when the police saw the bus pull up behind us it was like they said, ah, forget about it.

"Are they all with you?"

"Yes. They're coming with us."

"What are they?"

"Teachers and students."

"Those fuckers we *are* going to make get out."

So I said to the *compañero*: "Let's get out with our cameras." And so we got out of the truck with our cameras.

"No," the police all shouted. "No pictures!"

So in the end, they didn't make everyone on the bus get out. We all went through the checkpoint and drove to the place where the two students had been killed. When we got there the soldiers were there; there were two army trucks there. It was about one-thirty in the morning. One young guy was lying dead there in the road and the other one was back a bit near a workshop. One of the vans that the students had brought was all blown to pieces. There were another three trucks all shot up. And no one was there from the state detectives, the morgue, the police, nothing. When we got there, the first thing the teachers asked the soldiers ... because a student who I think had been there during the attack came up and said that they didn't know where some of the *compañeros* were, that the police had taken them off in their patrol trucks. Thrown in the beds of the trucks. So the teachers started asking the soldiers to start looking for the missing students. Mainly in the place called Barandillas, the city jail, where they take drunks and that kind of thing. Supposedly about forty of the students were there. But the authorities didn't look for them at the jail until the next day, around ten in the morning I think. We were there for a while and then went to the state courthouse. Students started arriving in about six trucks of the state investigative police; they had a whole bunch of students, the ones they were able to pick up in the streets. Up until six in the morning, when we left, I think a truck was still coming with students. But they never went to look in Barandillas. We were going to go back to Chilpancingo, but the federal police told us that we shouldn't go because some *sicarios* had blocked the road near Mezcala with cars and buses.

If you go right now to Zumpango you'll see the municipal police have set up checkpoints in the entrance and exits to town. Iguala was like that, or worse. Iguala has three access routes: toward Teloloapan, Taxco, and Chilpancingo. And on the old highway, every day, twenty-four hours a day, the police were always there.

SANTIAGO FLORES, 24, FRESHMAN. We got to the hospital and they put me on a stretcher in the operating room. When they laid me down I asked them where my *compañero* who had been shot in the head was. They said:

"We can't tell you." They were rushing around. I asked them multiple times where the guy who had been shot in the head was and they told me they didn't know. They injected me with something and I slept for a while. When I woke up there was a man, a bit heavyset, and a woman, a teacher. They said the man was a driver, but I don't know what kind of driver, or where he was from. They said that they were a driver and a teacher. They had shot the teacher in the back, I think. But when I saw her, she looked normal, like she was okay. She was talking normally. The man, he was in worse shape. Then they came up and closed the curtain so I couldn't see and they started operating on the man. When I asked the nurse again where he was, she said:

"Who? Your *compañero* with the buzz haircut, the little buzz-cut guy, the one who came just like you did?"

"Yes. Where is he?"

"Problem is, there are a number of you guys, quite a few, but there is one with a gunshot in the head."

"The one with the gunshot in the head. Where is he?"

"You'd better worry about yourself. The way you're going, with your lung problem, you could make it worse. You'd better worry about yourself. Your *compañero* is in critical condition. They are operating on him now. They are just now operating on him. He's in bad shape, between life and death. You'd better worry about yourself."

That was when I began to cry. I asked the nurse why they did this to us. The nurse left without answering me.

It was almost five in the morning. A child arrived, a boy. I knew he was a kid because I was listening, but I didn't open my eyes. I didn't want to see who it was. A woman was crying, she was wailing. She was asking why him. She was saying:

"My dear boy, why you?" She was saying: "My little boy, why God, why did you tear him away from here, away from me here?" She was speaking to the boy, asking him to open his little eyes, but he didn't open them. The boy had already died. I was just listening.

The woman was crying, wailing, for maybe fifteen or twenty minutes, talking to her son, saying goodbye to him. She was saying:

"My dear boy, I'll let you go in peace. I ask you one thing, close your little mouth. Close your little mouth." Because he died and his mouth was open. His mom was saying:

"I ask you to close your little mouth."

I feel like she was closing his mouth but then it would open again. The woman was weeping, me too, we were both sobbing, and she was saying:

"My little boy, just close your little mouth." That was the only thing she asked of him and, well, he couldn't close his mouth and it stayed open. I overheard the doctors saying:

"There aren't enough of us; there are some sixteen people with gunshot wounds; there are about sixteen of them and we can't handle them all." They said that the teacher and the driver both died.

ERICK SANTIAGO LÓPEZ, 22, SOPHOMORE. When I arrived, the hospital director asked me my name. I told him my name. Then he asked me where I was coming from. I told him that I am from the Ayotzinapa college.

"They should have killed you," he snarled, "fucking *ayotzinapo*." He didn't give me any medical attention. A military nurse attended to me. A military nurse told the doctors:

"I'll take care of the boy." Then they took off my clothes, leaving me just in my boxers, and took me to the operating area. Soon after, my *compa* Aldo arrived, and another freshman who got shot in the hand, and the guy who got shot in the mouth. There I was.

About two hours had gone by when the police came looking for me. Maybe they had been given the order to kill me because they showed up really aggressive, looking for me. I really am grateful to the nurse because she told them that I wasn't there anymore, that my *compañeros* had taken me out of the hospital, had taken me somewhere else. The police left.

MIGUEL ALCOCER, 20, FRESHMAN. No one talks about the other Estrella de Oro bus. We never heard anything about it again. When we were driving down that straight street in an Estrella de Oro bus, they say that the students on the other Estrella de Oro bus had gone a different route. And on that other route I heard that they had been speaking on the phone with our *compañeros* saying that they were on their way out of town, and they were asking where we were. A number of my *compañeros* had said that they were okay, on their way out of town. We never knew what happened to that bus. The *compañeros* on the Estrella Roja bus said they saw those *compañeros* in that other bus beneath an overpass and there were a bunch of police there. But no one talks about that bus. They say that it was all shot up, beneath the overpass, and there were a lot of police there. I think they also took students from that bus, I think that they are disappeared too.

JORGE, 20, FRESHMAN. Around five in the morning someone knocked on the door. We thought that they'd found us. Then the woman from the house called to us saying that it was a *compañero*. And, in fact, we recognized his voice. He said that the danger had passed and that the state police were going to take us. We all went outside and went with the state police. They took us walking back to where the buses were because, they said, they had left their patrol trucks there. We went walking toward the buses when we saw the two bodies of our *compañeros*, the *compañeros* that they had killed there.

JORGE HERNÁNDEZ ESPINOSA, 20, FRESHMAN. Around six in the morning I went to the taxi stand and got in a cab. I still didn't know anything about what had happened. I had just heard the shots. That morning I got to my hometown. A *compañero* called me and asked how I was.

"I'm okay," I said.

He told me that they had killed *Chino*, they had killed *Chilango*, and they had killed *Fierro*. That's what we called them. So then I started crying. Before that I hadn't cried at all, not once. I had just been scared, on edge, all that. It wasn't until that moment that I cried.

We had said to ourselves, okay, with the guys the police took there won't be any trouble: tomorrow or the day after tomorrow we'll go and get them out of jail, it won't be a problem. We never thought . . . The first thing that came to mind was that the police were taking them to jail. Tomorrow or the day after we'll get them out of jail. That they might beat them up, that they might torture them. But only that. We never thought, we never imagined that the police would disappear them. It was the twenty-eighth, that Sunday—because that Saturday the *compañeros* spent all day in Iguala giving declarations to state detectives and prosecutors and didn't go back to the college until that night—it wasn't until Sunday that they went to look for our *compañeros* in the jail and didn't find them.

ERNESTO GUERRERO, 23, FRESHMAN. They told us that the secretary general of the committee had gone back to the place where we had been attacked.

"I'm going," the teacher said.

"I'll go with you," I said.

But he took me to the state courthouse, because that's where we were taking refuge. The state assistant attorney general directed several state police squads to take us through the streets of Iguala, gathering our *compañeros* who had hidden. Everyone had tried to hide wherever they could: some in the brush; some, thank God, had been taken into houses, people had opened their houses to them. Others had hidden in barren fields. Everyone hid wherever they could. So the state police went out with *compañeros* to take everyone to the state courthouse so that we would be safe, in a safe place. We started giving our testimonies. The person at the courthouse who took my testimony asked me:

"And you all didn't shoot?"

"With what? Lend me your M-16. Let's arm ourselves and if we run into those bastards, they can try and kill me while I am defending myself. But we didn't even have rocks anymore. Now, how's that supposed to work?"

Even if we did have more rocks, bullets and rocks are not the same, they don't compare. I mean, it would be an unequal confrontation, and you can't call it a confrontation if the weapons are unequal. It really angered me that they would ask me that.

At seven in the morning they gathered five of us

together and said: "*Compañeros*, we need you to stay strong. We have a horrible picture to show you, something truly awful. We want you to tell us what you think." They showed a photo and we saw the *compañero* Julio César Mondragón, the guy we called *Chilango*. His face was cut off and his eyes were missing. When I saw it I honestly couldn't believe it. I couldn't believe that it was my *compañero*, my friend. They found him at seven in the morning about three blocks from where it all happened. What we think is that as he was trying to escape, they found him, and took him because the autopsy showed that they'd skinned his face while he was still alive. They removed the skin of his face while he was still alive and he was still screaming when they took out his eyes.

GERMÁN, 19, FRESHMAN. We got the news that they had found another body, a *compa* that we called *Chilango*. They cut off his face. They disfigured him. We just went into shock; we were traumatized, to tell the truth.

ALEX ROJAS, FRESHMAN. We left the house at around five in the morning. The *paisa* from the committee asked:

"Who was it last night who said they'd go look for the *compañeros*?"

"Me."

"If you want, go have a look now. Walk around and see what you see, but don't go too far, and be careful."

"Sure, no problem, I'll go."

And I left the house, alone, at around five in the morning. I walked up to the edge of the neighborhood. Up there it was pretty much hillside and wilderness. I started to walk around and was calling out for them, not too loudly, calling out their nicknames. A couple of men came out.

"Hey kid, what are you looking for?"

"I'm looking for some *compañeros* that came this way."

"Ah, okay. No, they're not here."

"Ah, okay, fine."

And there I was, calling out for them. I was walking around there looking for the *compañeros* for about twenty minutes. I had gone kind of far and then went back.

"I didn't see anyone," I told the *compañeros*. "There are a bunch of houses but I didn't see anyone. I was calling out for them, but they didn't answer me." So we went back down from that neighborhood. We went back down the way we had come up, chased by the police. Just like before, we were walking along Periférico and we saw another police truck. It braked. It was just one police truck and just stopped, we stopped too. Then it left. Then another federal police truck passed us. They just looked at us and kept going. And we were scared of the police trucks because we knew we couldn't trust anyone, not the police, because they had shot directly at us. The *paisa* called another *compa* who said that they were riding with the state investigative police.

"What? What is that? What do you mean?" the *paisa* said. "You're riding with the police? Don't you know they shot at us? That they were the ones who killed our *compañero*?"

But the other *compa* was saying no, we could trust these because they were sent by the attorney general's office. And just then, near Sam's Club we saw the police truck. It stopped about fifteen meters from us, and we were, well, scared. We didn't have anything. We started walking.

The police truck stopped, the driver put it in reverse, and the state investigative police began shouting at us.

"Boys, get in, your *compañeros* are with us, don't worry, get in, don't be afraid!"

We did not want to get in that truck. Then I looked and saw a *compañero* from the school and he waved to us to get in the back of the truck.

"*Paisa*'s in the truck," I said, "get in." *Paisa* was his nickname. We got in and were riding back there, scared, worried, hungry, tired, exhausted, and with the fear that they'd take us somewhere else.

ANDRÉS HERNÁNDEZ, 21, FRESHMAN. Two days later, when the list was published in the newspapers, the first list with fifty-seven disappeared, I was on that list. They thought I was disappeared. I called my brother at the school and asked him to tell everyone that I was okay, that I wasn't disappeared, that I was staying with my other brother. That's why the list got smaller, other *compañeros* also got in touch with the school.

RODRIGO MONTES, 32, JOURNALIST FROM IGUALA. He appeared Saturday morning. He had clear signs of torture. They had beaten him all around this part of his torso, his ribs. He had bruises all over his stomach, he had been hit there. It looked like they had been beating him, I don't know, with clubs, because the bruises went all the way across his ribs, from one side to the other. And surely you've already seen the image of how he was skinned.

IVÁN CISNEROS, 19, SOPHOMORE. It hit me hard when they showed me the photo of our *compa Chilango*. I was the one who recognized him.

"This *compa* is *Chilango*," I said. That's what I told them when they showed me the photo. I recognized him because he was a buddy of mine. He had told me his story. There were a lot of rumors about that guy. Some *compañeros* from Tenería said that he had been expelled from there. He had also been at Tiripetío.

At first they called him *Tenebrio*, the guy from Tenería. But I told the freshmen that he was no longer a *Tenebrio*, he was an *Ayotzinapa*.

"He's gonna be the *Chilango*," I said, "no more *Tenebrio*: I don't want to hear anyone call this guy *Tenebrio*, he's *Chilango*."

He had already told me that he had a baby girl and that he needed to go work to cover his family's expenses. I think he had a job as a security guard, I don't know where, but I think he worked with security in some way. He worked and helped support his family. What little he was able to make he gave to his family and came back here with just enough to pay for the trip. I told that *compa* that his past didn't matter here, that we weren't going to deny him the opportunity to study here. He made it through the trial week, he made it through it all. Here at the school he was really serious, but he also joked around, like you should.

He had asked for permission to go work because his wife had just gotten out of the hospital and he needed to earn a bit to provide for them. It's different having a family, so I supported that *compa*, I gave him permission. I remember well that he had asked for permission to go work that weekend. He told me that he needed to see his family, he needed to work for a few days. I told him no worries, man, it's all good. But he wanted to go before October 2.

"Look, let's do this," I said to him, "after the October 2 march you can go work, you can stay there in Mexico City and come back the following Sunday." Personally, I really feel bad about that *compa* because, in all honesty, how to say it: if he had gone in that moment. . . .

COYUCO BARRIENTOS, 21, FRESHMAN. A *compa* called us at around six in the morning. He asked where we were and told us that it was all over, that the student secretary general was with the state investigative police and a couple of soldiers. He told us to come out of hiding, that it was okay now. We asked the owners of the house if they could open the door for us and we thanked them for giving us shelter there. We left.

The guys on the roof came down; they were soaking wet. One guy had to take off the T-shirt he was wearing because he couldn't take the cold anymore. We met up with the other *compañeros*. The first thing I did was to ask who had been killed. The secretary confirmed that it was *Chino*. I didn't know what to think. I wanted to confirm it myself, to go see, but they told me that they had been taken to the morgue. It was during that time that I turned on my cell phone. When I was getting in the police truck I got a call from *Chino*'s cousin asking me how he was, asking if he was with me, how he was, what had happened. I couldn't say anything. Not a word came out. I didn't know what to say. I felt so powerless, so useless. His cousin kept asking me. He wanted to know. The only thing I said was that I was sorry, that I couldn't do anything.

"What the fuck," he said, almost crying. "Cut the bullshit!"

"I couldn't do anything, man," I said.

He kept asking me for Daniel. Until I told him that I'd been told that Daniel had been taken to the morgue. There was silence and then he hung up. The state police took us to the courthouse there in Iguala. When we got there his cousin called me again. I still didn't believe, didn't want to believe it, neither of us wanted to believe that it was Daniel. By then his cousin was crying; he asked me if it was true, if I had seen him myself. I said that I hadn't seen him, but that the secretary had confirmed it. If it had been up to me I would have gone back. One *compañero* told me that he had been standing next to Daniel and was able to see where he was lying in the street crying for help, and that he wanted to go back but those assholes were still shooting. He said that he saw Daniel with blood on his neck. I was very upset with that *compa*.

"Why didn't you tell me? If I had known, if I had seen, I wouldn't have given a fuck if they shot me, I would have gone back for him," I said.

While we were there at the courthouse, they gathered us together and started to compile information about what had happened. We shouldn't talk, the police couldn't do anything to us, they couldn't arrest us because this time we were the victims, we weren't guilty. We tried to calm ourselves down. It would all be over soon. My mind went blank. I didn't register what was happening all around me. I just saw the other *compañeros* getting called over to give their testimonies. They took them into some offices and they took a while to come back out. The other *compañeros* were waiting in this big room. I didn't want to give my testimony. I was far from all of them. I didn't want to have anything to do with all that.

When things calmed down a bit I got another call from one of Daniel's other cousins. This cousin is older than both Daniel and myself and is an Ayotzinapa graduate. He called to ask about Dani. Like I tell my *compañeros*, it takes a serious set of balls, and held tight, to give news like that. I don't wish that on anyone. And that cousin told me not to lose my grip, that it wasn't my fault, that if I couldn't have done anything, then there was nothing I could do. He said that things happen for a reason and that their family had my back.

We were all waiting for the *compañeros* to finish with their testimonies. Everything was quiet. In the distance you could hear the voices of some secretaries, workers there at the courthouse asking questions, taking notes, running around. And I want to express my gratitude to a social worker, a woman who was supporting us, lifting our spirits, from the moment we arrived there.

"Stay strong, boy, don't let these animals see you cry," she told me. "Show them you are braver than they are; these animals don't deserve to see you all cry."

The sun came up. We still couldn't process what was happening. People started moving around a lot, going in and out of the waiting room area. The *compañeros* in charge were running here and there asking who was missing, who was wounded, who was there, how many of us had left. I walked outside. I had heard that someone was going to identify the bodies. I went to ask the secretary:

"Are you going to the morgue?"

"Yes."

"I don't give a fuck. I'm going with you."

He looked at me for a second and then said: "Alright man, I'll let you know in just a minute."

We were waiting for the authorities to take us. It took them a little while. A couple of *compañeros* bought some things to eat and were sharing them with all of us. Then some agents showed up asking if we wanted to go identify the police, the ones who had attacked us; they said they had located all their squad trucks. They just wanted us to go point them out, so that it would be legitimate. Of all the *compañeros* who had already given their testimonies, no one wanted to go. Another *compañero*, a sophomore, came over to us.

"We have to go identify those fuckers, because we can't just let this go," he said. "If we don't identify them now, they'll be back. And then the deaths and the disappearance of the *compañeros* will all have been in vain."

"I'll go," I said.

We talked to some other *compañeros* who decided to go as well. We got ready and they took us to the police station. They explained to us that we would go in to identify them. We were waiting for them to bring all the police officers together. We got into a state police truck with the windows rolled up; we wore ski masks. In the entrance to the police station parking lot we saw one of the police trucks that we had pelted with rocks to repel the attack. Then we saw the rest of the trucks toward the back of the lot. Others were not there. We got out of the truck and everyone stared at us; they didn't know what was happening. They took us into a room, behind a window with Venetian blinds. They made all the police at the station walk by us; they called out the names and the number of their squad trucks of all the police that were on duty that night. Right away, we were able to identify one of the police, the first one. The minute we identified him a state detective came up to us and said that the one we identified was the municipal police station chief.

The state detective told us that this guy and the director of the municipal police were tied to . . . that they were the ones who did whatever they pleased in Iguala. The state police had been watching them, but couldn't do anything until we identified them, he said. But then he told us very clearly that the only one they could do anything to was the station chief, not the director. He said that they were connected to the DIF director and the *sicarios*. We kept identifying the other police officers. At first we were able to identify nineteen. Then they brought the others who were in the same patrol trucks. Then we left. We went back to the courthouse and were there all day.

JUAN PÉREZ, 25, FRESHMAN. Honestly, I couldn't sleep because I saw how my *compañero* went down; I saw how they shot him in the head; I saw how he fell close to me. His body was right here. He went down, went down: that moment stayed in my mind all night and I couldn't sleep. I stayed awake. I imagined that he was still right there.

ALEX ROJAS, FRESHMAN. They gave us a cup of coffee and a piece of bread. That was the only thing we'd eaten since the day before. We were all tired and scared. You could see the sadness and worry on all the *compañeros'* faces. A woman, I don't know what her position was there at the courthouse, came in.

"We have information that there are some young men near the highway that goes to Tierra Caliente," she told us. "We want to go pick them up and bring them back here, but we need some of you to go with us so that they'll trust us and will want to get in the police trucks and come back here."

They had started to look for everyone like that since early in the morning, perhaps four or four-thirty in the morning. They started looking for *compañeros* in different parts of the city. Some were near the bridge, others were in some other place, and that's how they went about finding and picking everyone up. After a while, maybe around seven or eight, we didn't hear anything else about the others.

There was supposedly a brigade of state police out looking for more *compañeros*, but no one else came; they said they couldn't find any more students. Since it was possible that more *compañeros* were hiding, the secretary asked the state investigative police, the ones in charge there, how many students had been arrested, because we clearly saw the municipal police arrest our *compañeros*. They called Barandillas, the Iguala jail, and the people there said they didn't have any information about any arrested students. That was when the concern, the question came up: where are our *compañeros*? If the municipal police clearly put the students in their patrol trucks and arrested them: where were they? We started making a list of everyone at the courthouse. A number of *compañeros* were giving their testimonies. There were a number of *compañeros* with bullet wounds, or wounds where bullets had grazed them. One student had a graze wound on his foot, another across his chest, another on his arm and another, I think, on his knee. That's when the uncertainty hit us.

We made the list and started adding everything up and there were like fifty-seven *compañeros* missing, or more, sixty-four I think were the ones missing at that point. Time went by as we tried to see who was really missing. We knew that some *compañeros* had received permission to go home and they were in their houses. There were some other *compañeros* who had stayed back at the school to finish up things they had to do, and they didn't go with us to Iguala. That's when the number went down to fifty-seven *compañeros*.

We stayed there at the courthouse pretty much all that day. Teachers and other people went to support us; they took us food and we ate there. We were all afraid, we didn't want to be there in Iguala. With all that had happened, we did not want to be there. We knew that even with all these police around, it was not safe at the courthouse; they can show up anywhere and strafe us with machine guns again.

So then the human rights people arrived and asked us if we could tell them what had happened. Four of us went into an office and started writing down everything that had happened, each of us on our own. We were there working on that when they came looking for me and another *compa*. They had to go inspect the different locations where everything had happened and they wanted a *compañero* who had been near the overpass where the other students were attacked, and another *compañero* who had been near the mini Aurrera where pretty much the worst attack happened, the machine-gun attack against the *compañeros*. They wanted us to go with them.

I asked a *paisa* from the committee if I could go.

"Yes, you can," he said, "you all can go in just a moment; eat something and then you can go."

We went with another *paisa* from the committee. We went to the curving ramp that leads down to the highway that goes under the overpass, but the bus wasn't there anymore. Someone had taken it. The only thing we found was a bunch of broken glass. And in the distance it looked like the grass was all smashed flat and there were a bunch of cut tree branches. One of the human rights guys asked:

"Why did they cut these branches? Did they torture guys with these? Did they beat them with these as clubs, or what happened?"

The lowest branches were all cut and all the sticks were lying around.

PVC, 19, FRESHMAN. We went to the state courthouse there in Iguala to give our testimonies. We got there; they told us to all go in and give our testimonies. Then some people from Iguala went to support us, they took us food. More *compañeros* kept coming, and kept coming. They were among the ones who had been all dispersed throughout the city hiding; the state police were going around picking them up. And we asked about the *compañeros* that had been taken away in the police trucks, if they were really under arrest, or at some police station. And they told us no, that the *compañeros* were not under arrest and that they seemed to be disappeared. They said the police trucks that took them had never arrived at the police station to make a formal arrest. We tried to call them on their cell phones . . . but no, no one answered, all the calls went straight to voice mail, straight to voice mail, or the phones were turned off. A little later the secretary started moving around, doing what he had to do, investigating what had happened with the students who had been arrested and the ones we hadn't heard anything from.

That's how we spent the hours. The *compañeros* out there had been disappeared, and we wanted to get out of that place, because it was truly horrifying what we had lived through there.

CHAPARRO, 20, FRESHMAN. We got the news sometime around noon. They told us that they had just found a *compañero*, and he had been tortured. They beat him, took out his eyes, and cut off his face and ears. That is when the terror hit us. No one knew what to do. Around then we also realized that some parents were starting to arrive asking where their sons were. It was simply too sad to tell them that we didn't know where they were, or that they had been killed. We couldn't do it; we didn't know how, more than anything, how to tell them. What we would say was: "Forgive us, ma'am, but we don't know your son," or "I don't know him."

The truth was that we did know him, but we didn't want to tell his parents that he couldn't be found. It's unsettling, it is so sad to tell them that their sons are nowhere to be found, and their sons are our *compañeros*. One woman, who is from my hometown and a relative of mine, asked me about her son. The woman had just lost her husband. We really didn't want to tell her that her son wasn't there, that we didn't know where he was. The woman, upon realizing that her son wasn't there with us, went outside to be alone, not to be around the parents who were finding their sons. She stood apart from everyone else. She took out a lime and cut it. She is diabetic. She went to cut open a lime and drink its juice.

JOSÉ ARMANDO, 20, FRESHMAN. We got back to the college. A lot of parents were here at the school; everybody's parents were already here waiting on the basketball court. Many of them found their sons, they found us. The parents of the disappeared wept that day when they saw that their sons hadn't come back with us. They kept asking us questions.

"And my son? And my son?"

"We don't know, *tía*, the police took them, but they weren't at any jail or anything."

That's when the nighmare here began, the nightmare

of the disappeared *compañeros*. But I'm going to tell you something: in spite of that we're still here. A lot of *compañeros* grabbed their things and went back to their houses that very day.

"I'm leaving," they said. "What can I do here? I survived one nightmare, why would I look for another one? No."

They went back home and to this day haven't returned. My parents also told me to go back home.

"What would you both do," I asked them, "if I were disappeared? Because I was there too and I could have been disappeared just like my *compañeros*. They could have taken me. What would you all do? Would you really want my *compañeros*, all of them, to just walk away like nothing happened, just like that?"

Because, you know, we all got along well. We were like brothers, sharing everything, working together, laughing together, and fucking around. Sure, sometimes we fought, but they are our brothers because that's how we're taught to share here. And so I'm going to stay in the struggle. I'm never going to forget my *compañeros* who fell that night, or those who are disappeared. You can't say that they are dead; they are not dead, and they are going to live in our hearts forever. And if the government thought that it would be able to do away with this school just like that, if they thought that this would terrorize us even more and lead to the school being lost, well, they were very wrong. The government is making a big mistake.

COYUCO BARRIENTOS, 21, FRESHMAN. When we got to the school, I went to Dani's room. His mom and dad were there. I couldn't find the words to tell them the news.

I didn't want it to be me who would confirm what had happened to them. When his parents saw me . . . his mom burst into tears. The only thing I could do was to embrace her and ask for her forgiveness for not taking care of him like we would have wished. When things calmed down a bit, his dad asked me if I was going to continue or leave the school. I had been thinking since that night that no matter what happened, I was going to continue.

"Think about it hard," he told me, "what is about to happen is not going to be easy."

"Maybe I won't stay here for myself," I answered, "but I'm going to stay here for Dani. He didn't deserve what they did to him. And also for my *compañeros* who are disappeared. We have to find them."

EMILIANO NAVARRETE, FATHER OF JOSÉ ÁNGEL NAVARRETE GONZÁLEZ, 18, FRESHMAN. I was at home, resting. It was around ten-thirty at night. My wife would usually call our boy at night. In fact, he had gone to the house just the day before. I remember talking with him; I liked the changes I was seeing in him. Like any eighteen-year-old, sometimes he doesn't want to help with tasks at home. It's natural for an eighteen-year-old. Well, it seemed like he was trying to change some things in his life. He would come home from the college and start sweeping, or cleaning the furniture. That day I gave him a hug and I said:

"You know what, son? I'll come looking for you no matter where you are, I'll find you." I never thought that it would be the next day. I never thought that something would happen, that they would be attacked in Iguala. Well, it was the day of twenty-sixth. As I said, my wife usually called him. I was in the living room watching TV. Then I heard our son Pepe tell my wife that the police were attacking them.

"Hand me the phone," I said to my wife, "let me talk to him." She passed me the phone and I said to Pepe, my son: "Pepe, what's happening?" You could hear a bunch of screaming through the phone, a lot of boys shouting.

"Dad, the police here in Iguala are attacking us. They shot my friend in the head, he's lying in the street and something smells really bad."

"Son, try to hide, to escape."

What the smell was, I don't know what he was referring to. Maybe tear gas? Or maybe the bus tires had been blown out? I never imagined that the police were attacking them with guns! I thought the police were attacking them maybe with clubs or tear gas, that's what I thought!

Then that was it. The call was cut off, and I didn't hear anything else. But it didn't even pop into my mind that they were being attacked with firearms. That night a car from the college came driving through the streets here, through Tixtla, announcing that there were problems at the school, that the boys had been attacked. But they didn't say anything about guns. I thought that the police . . . just wanted to stop them from taking the buses that they were going to use for October second.

So the hours went by and we didn't know what was happening. It wasn't till the next day that a number of us parents decided to go to Iguala to find out what was happening. About five of us got together before dawn and left for Iguala. I got to Iguala and went to the courthouse thinking that my boy would be there. I got to the courthouse and saw a whole bunch of kids there. I think something like a hundred and fifteen students were in Iguala that night.

I still hadn't realized that they had been attacked with

firearms! So I started asking for my son. I saw that some of them were already giving testimony in some offices and others were outside. So, since they were freshmen, I guess they didn't all know each other that well; they had just been there for two months. And since they get divided into sections, it isn't so easy for them all to get to know each other so quickly. I asked a young man if he had seen my son and he asked me what my son's name is.

"Well, his name José Ángel," I said, "but we call him Pepe." The boys there said no.

"But, go look inside," they told me, "there are a bunch of boys inside."

I walked all throughout the place. Then they told me that some of the boys had been arrested and taken to the city jail, a place they call Barandillas.

So I left. I went into Iguala, toward the center of Iguala, near the bus station. I went walking through the streets thinking that they could be around there lost, or hiding inside a house. That's more or less what I imagined. I didn't know, I still didn't understand the reality of what had happened. I looked for him all day. I looked together with another *compañero*. We looked all through the center of Iguala, but we didn't find anyone, nothing. We went back to the courthouse where all the boys were. There were some people telling the secretary if they wanted to go back to the college, the ones who were safe. They said they would get some buses and a police convoy to guard them back to Ayotzinapa. I didn't want to return to the school until they brought our sons back to us. But the secretary of the students here said that he was going. And so we all came back.

My thought was to stay there until they gave us our sons, and then we could all come back. The right thing to do, I think, was stay there. We should have stayed there until they brought us our sons. The government would have looked for them that very afternoon. For me, that was something I never liked, I'll tell you, that we came back to the school then.

The following day was a Sunday. Two or three other parents and I starting going out looking in the hillsides and along the highways. We drove all around in a small pickup looking for our sons. We had heard that some of the students had run into the hillsides—at that point we had realized that they had been attacked with guns! We knew that the government had straight up shot at them with machine guns, maybe they meant to wipe them out with all those bullets.

We didn't understand why they had done it. Today we still have many questions, so many questions. We have looked for our sons. The first two weeks we looked for them on our own. We were just parents looking without any results, alone, looking along the highways, in the wilderness. Sometimes we went out to where there are caves or abandoned mines and things like that. After about two weeks the federal police came and started looking with us. Well, first we met with the federal government in Chilpancingo. That's where we held the meetings. There we told them that, as parents, we wanted to participate in the searches and to be able to use the information that we had to guide the searches with the federal police accompanying us. Besides the marches, I've preferred to look for information. I feel much better going out to look for my boy, for all the boys, wherever they may be. That has kept me a bit stronger.

We have gone so many places, often with the federal police. When we would get information we would go out with them. We would go out to the places we'd heard they might be, but sadly without positive results. A lot of people take advantage of us, take advantage of our pain, giving us false information, like those people who read tarot cards. One of them told me once. . . . I didn't know anything about those kinds of people, but I realized what was going on when he asked me for money to give me information. And believe me, in such desperation I fell for it. He told me that our boys were in Iguala, near the hill known as La Parota. I remember going out there with the help of the federal government. I went out there to a house where our boys supposedly could be found. The tarot card guy said he'd send me a text message when I got near there to give me a more precise location. None of it was true. I never received a text message from that person. The only thing I know is that he took advantage of our situation to take from us the little bit of money that we don't even have.

I've gone on so many search expeditions and marches. I've gone to other states to inform people about what's happening so that they can keep supporting us in our demand for our sons. Because here we know that the government knows perfectly well where they are, because it was the government that took them. They have offered I think a million pesos for information. And how is it that no one knows anything? I can tell you that no one knows because the government has known from the beginning. The government knows where the government took them: that's why there is no information! If it had been, as they say here, the bad guys who took them, trust me, we'd know by now. Someone would have claimed that money the government is offering, or would have demanded a ransom. The government puts up a large amount of money asking for information because it knows that no one is going to claim that money because the government already knows everything. They know where the boys are. That night that they did everything: it was completely planned and coordinated. The municipal police coordinated with federal police and soldiers to cordon off the city and not let anyone escape.

They were the ones in control that night, no one else. So I always come to the conclusion that the government knows where they are. And what pisses me off, believe me, is that we don't even know why they're keeping them. The government says that supposedly they were confused for a criminal group called Los Rojos, The Reds. Listen: if a crimminal group had really been on board those buses they would not have been unarmed. Please! Those people are always armed, they would have killed some police officers! It is completely false to try and link our sons to those types of people. This government has not taken us seriously. From the beginning they have not investigated anyone. They've only released the testimony of that thug *Cepillo* who says they went to burn the students in Cocula.

I didn't hear his testimony. I was not in the room listening to his testimony. Not one of our lawyers was in the room listening when they made that person testify. Only those who were there know what happened.

How can we believe them? How are we going to trust them when it is the very same government that is doing this very horrible damage to us?

We absolutely do not believe what the government says. They want to wash their own hands of all this using other people, using people who are outlaws.

We want truly serious results. We know that our sons are alive. There was no huge fire like that person says. Some of the boys say they were still being chased at three in the morning. They were just trying to get back together with their *compañeros*.

So when did they supposedly start this big fire? That night it rained.

Where did they get enough wood at that hour of night? The residents of Cocula say there is no wood to be found around that area. How was it possible? It's not credible. The residents say plainly that there was no huge fire! They had burned people in previous years, but not that night. The government is lying: it is that simple.

How could it be possible that there was this enormous fire and yet afterward they found little chicken bones there? How is a little chicken bone going to survive that fire, survive a temperature supposedly so high that it completely incinerated the bones of the boys? For us, what they are saying is completely false.

There are many things that don't make sense. Supposedly they found forty-two bullet shells from a twenty-two-caliber pistol, and one nine-millimeter shell. And yet in the testimony of this Mr. Cepillo, he says that fifteen of the boys arrived suffocated to death. So they decided to kill them again? Why did they find exactly forty-three bullet shells?

The government wants to wash its hands of this and blame other people. We definitely think that it was the government that went back that night, without uniforms, returned with face masks and without uniforms to shoot at the students again. For us, this is all a bunch of lies. And believe me, it makes me mad as a father, as a simple, working person: we know the truth!

We know the truth, but who is going to help us face down this piece-of-shit government? We thought that when the federal government got involved we'd have positive results—that is, that we'd receive the support we needed so badly. But now I realize that we came to stand face to face with the enemy. Why? Because the government has been cruel to us, the parents, with the pure idiocies that old, bald Murillo Karam, the Attorney General, was spouting.

We still demand they bring us back our boys alive, because the police took them alive. They are alive, and darn it, I say we can come to an understanding as human beings through dialogue, but apparently this government has no human feelings. It has no feelings. The way this government has walked all over us is clear for all to see. I would never have thought that this government would be such a liar! I have never met people with such a capacity to lie so cruelly and still go around the world with their heads held high, visiting other countries like this president does, like nothing were happening in his country.

As parents what can we do? Horribly, they have our sons in their hands and we don't know how they are treating them. Because, believe me, this is painful, to think how they are treating them. I'm out here. I can drink water. I can eat. I can do whatever I like. But my son? And that knocks me flat; thinking about that sends me to the floor.

Dear God, why does such evil exist in the adult human? And your own government! Your own country!

We will keep struggling, demanding that they give us back our sons alive. I will always demand that the government give me my son. I want him back home because it hurts me to see his two siblings waiting for him. During that whole time I would get home at night, and I didn't want to go inside. I tried to get back after two in the morning so my other kids would be asleep and not see me. But believe me, my poor children were awake at two in the morning waiting for me: it hurt me to see them! It hurt me to see and know that another day had passed, and they were waiting for me to bring them good news about their brother, that

I had found him. Believe me, it's a heavy pain that clamps down on your heart. You feel powerless. You feel alone. At times you want to fall. This government doesn't just hurt you as a father or mother, it hurts your whole family, all your children. It sends your life into a tailspin. You abandon everything to hold onto the one hope that we find our sons. But the worthless government has never wanted to give us serious answers. Quite the opposite: it has treated us very badly, as if we were face-to-face with an enemy.

We will keep struggling, demanding they give us back our sons, with the help now of the experts. I think the experts represent a high card, the last card for me that we can play legally. After this there won't be any more. And believe me, I will not stop until they give me my son.

This government will have to pay for what it has done.

LUZ MARÍA TELUMBRE CASARRUBIAS, MOTHER OF CHRISTIAN ALFONSO RODRÍGUEZ TELUMBRE, 19, FRESHMAN. More than anything, you should know that this boy doesn't have an ounce of meanness in him. His dream is to pursue his studies and be able to help others. We are a very humble family, we struggle day by day to make ends meet. And he really loves his sisters, his three sisters. My four children have always worked hard. They are all studying. And I think that he, even though he's missing—but I know he is okay—has continued to motivate his sisters; and I know he is going to come back and keep fighting for his dreams, to become what he's always wanted to be.

He is a very easygoing child. He has always worked to do good, he's always been like that. He really likes dance. He actually didn't want to be a teacher. But considering our financial situation, well, he decided to study here at the college to be able to help us out. But he wanted to be an agricultural engineer. But without the resources and money, he couldn't be what he wanted to be. He really likes dance.

"I'm going straight to Bellas Artes, mom. I think I can make it," he'd say. "I like to hear the audience's applause. I like people to admire me when I get up on stage."

He is like that. He always liked things like that, sharing his joy with people; he was always like that. He started developing his passion for dance when he started middle school. His dance group is called Xóchitl. And he has performed all over. He even went to Mexico City to perform. And around here they've gone everywhere, during all kinds of events. Here in Tixtla whenever there are meetings for the various saint's days, he always goes to the meetings. He really likes dancing. Nothing else.

"Hey son," his father would say every once in a while, "would you like to play some sport like basketball or soccer?"

"No, dad," he would answer, "I don't like that stuff. I like dance. I feel like that's why my feet are here, to dance."

And even when he's home he practices with his sisters; they also know how to dance really well. You know, even little kids in the neighborhood would come by and say:

"Hey everyone, come over here, Christian is dancing."

Christian would put on his dancing boots and dance with his sisters and he would start up a fandango right there with his sisters. Sometimes even women here from the neighborhood would come by and follow his steps. And he will keep dancing, because some day he'll come and accomplish his dreams.

He has really agile feet. He doesn't listen to any music other than *zapateado*, dance music for tap dancing–like steps. His sisters also know how to dance that music because they have studied it too. Especially the youngest, who's now in middle school, she's the one who dances the most.

Christian said that he felt really happy because, well, we don't have much money. One time I paid three hundred pesos so that my youngest daughter could rent the costumes she needed for the school's anniversary. Christian told me, that it was all worth what we paid.

"Mom," he said to me, "your effort was worth it; my little sister dances with such elegance, I really admire her. I like how she dances, her flow. . . . I think she was the best one out there. My little sister really knows how to dance that music, mom."

Sometimes they would have fandangos in the house with a little music player. He'd ask me if he could turn on some music.

"Yes," I'd say, "but not too loud." He always liked to turn the music as high as it would go. He also liked to shout, and you could hear him way out on the street corner. And that's how a lot of people would realize that he was starting to dance, and they'd come and lean in the doorway to watch.

"Come on in! If you like, dance with me," he'd say.

He is an easygoing kid. He doesn't start trouble with anyone. Everyone on our street loves him, and we love him. He really liked to go to the river, to the pools. He enjoyed playing in the mud. He liked being in the country more than in the city. He was raising pigs, rabbits, and hens, he really liked that. He has a guinea pig that looks like a big mouse; I call it Rat. It's still there, really fat. It's female. After Christian started here at the college he couldn't keep going out to feed his animals; now they're gone. But he's always really liked all that, animals.

We have a plot of land, but we only use it for some fruit trees. We have some limes, guavas, and plums. And we have some pigs out there that we've had for a long time. We only have a few trees; they're just for our consumption. I sell tortillas I make by hand. And sometimes we have tortillas left over, and so at least not to lose that investment of the tortillas, we use them to feed the pigs that we have. That's why we have the pigs.

Before that happened, the night of the twenty-sixth, we worked every day, including Sundays. It takes a lot to provide for my four children. I had to work every day of the week including Sundays. But now, since that happened on the twenty-sixth up to today, I haven't worked. I've been here at the school, in the marches, wherever they send me I've gone.

My husband, my daughter and my sister come with me. Only the two youngest stay home. I don't want to put them at risk, since we sometimes travel to other regions, or we travel at night. The last thing I'd want is for something to happen to them. Sometimes we get back late at night. Sometimes they don't tell us where we're going, we just show up somewhere where we find a lot of bad things. And the last thing I want is for something else to happen to my daughters.

My husband sells jugs of potable water. He makes very little. The minimum. He goes to the purification plant and buys the water jugs there for five pesos. Then he sells them for ten or twelve pesos, depending. When people have paid deposits on the jugs, then he sells it cheaper. But he has to earn at least a little bit. Sometimes business goes well, and sometimes the water is expensive and it goes poorly.

On the twenty-fifth, my son went to spend a little bit of time with us at the house. They had just started giving the students permission to leave the campus. He came home and told us that he might get permission to leave that Friday, the twenty-sixth. They were going to let them go home that

Friday. We took him back to the school at around six-thirty on the evening of the twenty-fifth.

Around ten o'clock at night on the twenty-sixth they told us that there were some problems at the school and that the parents needed to go to campus. It was urgent. So we had to come. Well, we were hoping they could have hidden in the hillsides, or in someone's house, someone who offered them help. All day Saturday and Sunday we waited for them. By Monday we were still, I was still terribly sad because they still had not identified the young man who by Monday was still at the morgue. They called that boy's mother asking for her to come identify him. It wasn't until Monday that they ruled out the possibility of that boy being the son of the other mothers.

Well, I've had a bad experience with the authorities. Up to now they have not answered our requests. I don't know if it's because we're poor, or because they simply haven't done anything yet. Because I think that if it were their children, they'd already be back home with them. In less than a day they'd be back with their parents. And we've already been waiting . . . and without any answers from the authorities. And what's more, they haven't investigated Aguirre. For example, we went to Mexico City to speak with President Enrique Peña Nieto, but he hasn't responded to any of the things we asked him. Supposedly we signed an agreement, but it hasn't been honored. That agreement we signed has never meant anything for us. If it had meant something, he would have taken action and would have responded to the things we asked him.

For example, they supposedly detained twenty-some-thing police officers. They took them all away from here to Nayarit, I don't know where, somewhere else, to another jail, to do their investigation. You'd think that if they commited the crime here, they should be judged here. There's no reason to take those police somewhere else, especially out of state. They should be judged here. Like we said one day to the Attorney General, Murillo Karam, let us talk to them for at least an hour, let's see what we can find out, if we can't get the truth out of them.

It isn't fair that we parents are the only ones suffering so much with the uncertainty of not knowing where our sons are, not knowing if they've eaten, if they get to sleep, if they've had a bath. All of that ruins us as parents. It ruins us because we don't know what's happening with our sons. And more than anything, for me, even though our family is humble . . . he's a boy dedicated to his family, to doing good. He doesn't have a mean bone in his body.

I, as a mother, know my son, and it's not okay that this is happening here in this country. There is no justice in it. Taking away a piece of the path my son has to walk. I feel like his steps are still incomplete. . . . I can't find a way to explain how I feel as a mother.

Yes, I've dreamt of him. At first I dreamt that he arrived, that he was at his aunt's house and I went by to whisper in his ear for him to pray a lot, that prayer would help him. And then I came back and went to the market. And every little while I told him:

"Pray a lot, it will help you, you know how to pray."

After that I dreamt of him again, but that he was already dead. I didn't see him, but someone told me I had to go claim him at the morgue. And I went through a door and came through to some kind of big trailer, and then I came out the trailer's door. I screamed desperately, asking for help, that it was not him, that they were lying to me telling me he was at the morgue. That's how I dreamed of him.

I feel that he is going to come home, and we are waiting

for him here. I don't feel like he isn't alive anymore. I feel that he is alive and is going to show up any minute.

MARIO CÉSAR GONZÁLEZ CONTRERAS, FATHER OF CÉSAR MANUEL GONZÁLEZ HERNÁNDEZ, 19, FRESHMAN, IN FRONT OF THE GOVERNOR'S OFFICE, CHILPANCINGO, 4 OCTOBER 2014. A million pesos are what our sons' lives are worth? That's what he spends on a drinking binge. That fucking pig. That wretch. We have an incompetent as governor.

"I can't answer you," Governor Ángel Aguirre said, and got up to leave.

"Are you at a loss for words, to answer me?"

We are exhausted. We are parents. We are already exhausted. We don't know what to do or whom to ask for help. And they send us that. . . . Well, I don't know how they could bring us all together to come here, and we are still idiotic enough to come for an audience with the governor. I don't know. Supposedly Peña Nieto wanted to change this country and who knows what else. . . . Why isn't he here now? Why is he not here? They are forty-three. They are students. And, unfortunately, like I said to the governor, lucky it's not his son, because in half an hour they would have found him. And without a scratch.

Our only crime is being poor and looking for a school where we can support our children. It's horrible, but that's how things are.

My son is César Manuel González Hernández. But I'm not here just for him. I'm here for all of them, because they were his *compañeros*. I don't know why people talk so badly about Ayotzinapa. I've been living at the school for a week and they are some beautiful boys, people who take the bread from their mouths to give it to the parents, kids who go without eating so that the parents can have a meal. I am from Tlaxcala. I am from Tlaxcala, *señores*. I've come to find out about all the filth they have here.

They let us into the meeting, *señores*, and they make us, the parents, go through a metal detector. How is it possible that they make us go through a metal detector? Make your system, your police, your killers go through the metal detector. What can we do to him? No, I didn't just take it, *señores*, not this time, I didn't take it. I don't know if that dog will have me killed. Let him do it. Here I am. But give me back my son. Nothing else. And the other forty-two students. That is all I ask.

I don't know why they kicked me out of the meeting. I am from Huamantla, Tlaxcala. We are good people. People who won't just sit and take it. People with enough balls . . . those sons of bitches. I told him that to his face, that son of a bitch, and I shut him up. He couldn't say a word to answer me, the idiot. What wretched people, truly. What fucking cowards, using guns. I wish one of those pimp sons of fucking bitches would say to me:

"You know what, let's go at it, you and me, son of a bitch, with our bare hands." I don't give a fuck. And still with his little smirk and "good evening." I just looked at him. He looked back at me.

"Yes? Tell me."

"What do you want me to tell you? Good evening? For you. For us with our guts tied in knots, with our guts a fucking wreck. . . . Our only fucking crime is being too poor to send our kids to a private school. Lucky it's not your son. They'd find your son in less than half an hour, you asshole, and without a fucking scratch. Or your car. Let's not talk about your son, let's talk about your goddamned car.

If someone were to steal it, in less than half an hour they'd bring it right back to you. And these sons of bitches, asslicking sons of dogs, standing there protecting you with their earphones, sons of fucking bitches, ball-licking motherfuckers. They do that because they don't know how to work, the assholes."

Does he want to kill me? Let him do it. He wants to kill me? Let him do it. I don't care. I care more about my son's life.

MARIO CÉSAR GONZÁLEZ CONTRERAS, FATHER OF CÉSAR MANUEL GONZÁLEZ HERNÁNDEZ, 19, FRESHMAN, HIGHWAY BLOCKADE PROTEST, CHILPANCINGO, 5 OCTOBER 2014. He is a cynical person. I asked him a lot of questions, and do you know what he said to me:

"Okay, so I'll get up and leave?"

"So you, sir, are standing up because you don't have any answers? You're incapable of providing us with answers? Why didn't you start the searches on Sunday, or Monday? Why?"

"Weren't we searching?"

"Lies. I left Tlaxcala at one-thirty in the morning, alone. And I don't care if they could have killed me. If they want to kill me, they can give me back my son, kill me and there's no problem. It is unjust that his forty-two *compañeros* are disappeared. You don't know the pain we feel. You don't know that we are physically, morally, and economically destroyed. Unfortunately, we don't have any money."

We want some certainty. They're telling us there are ten dead bodies in Taxco, there are twelve bodies over there. Now they've found two mass graves. And so now you're going to give us those bodies, all charred, all foul? I say, no sir. You all took them alive, and alive you have to bring them back to us. It wasn't some criminal organization that took them, and we're supposed to think they've already been killed. It was the police who took them! So, precisely what kind of security do they have here in Guerrero? You'd think the police follow the orders of their superiors, meaning they don't act on their own. I've been living here at the school for a week, during which time I've come to learn about all kinds of corruption here in Guerrero. And I say, how is it possible that the citizens—I'm not talking about the representatives of the law, but the citizens—how is it possible that as citizens people allow this kind of a situation? I mean, if people know perfectly well what is happening, damn it! Act!

Now they are just lying to us. They are driving us parents insane. We don't even know what to do, we don't know where to go. Ask me if a single authority has introduced themselves to us, has come up to us to say I am so-and-so and I'm here to help you with anything you need. No one has come to us. We, unfortunately, are not from here and we don't know anyone. We don't know whom to ask for help. We don't know. We are walking with our eyes closed.

"Mr. Governor," I told him last night, "I'm not here to get involved in politics, I just want my son. I didn't send my son to rob from anyone. I didn't send him to become a crook. I sent him to study. And for sending our sons to study, you're going to give me his dead body? How is that okay? That is not right. I don't think it's fair that as a father I didn't want my son to suffer the same hardships as me and sent him to study, and so you give him to me dead. That is not right. Until the final consequences, wherever life takes me, I have to find my son. I have to take him back to our home state. Because it is not right. It is not just. Unfortunately we have already been here for a week, and I thank the students who gave us a bit of clothing, soap, and food. And it is food that they need, food that they give to us, food that we're pretty much taking out of their mouths."

That Friday my son called me at three in the afternoon. I was sick with typhoid. He said:

"Dad, how are you?"

"Fine, fine, son."

"No, you sound bad. I'm going to ask for permission to go visit. I want to see you."

"No, son. You went to study. I want you to study hard."

He said that perhaps he'd come visit me, but I said no, horribly, I told him no. That was the worst mistake of my life, a mistake I cannot forgive myself for. But I told him: "You know what, I sent you off to study, buddy, and I want you to be someone in life." Yes, it's really intense. Very, very intense. We don't know if they went to plant bodies there. I swear, based on the things I've come to learn, it's very likely. That's what we can expect from the authorities. And that's what I don't understand about Mr. Peña Nieto: he said he was going to change the country. And unfortunately, I think everything is the same, the same; we're still in the same situation. The government says that they found thirteen of them. Lies.

The forty-three disappeared students are still disappeared. Not one of them has come back. So what is this? Are we supposed to just stay here thinking that they've already been killed? People are so cowardly now. Why do they burn people? Why do they dismember people? The governor offered a million pesos. That is a mockery. A million pesos gets him drunk. That's what one of his drinking binges costs.

You look over here, you find dead people. You look over there, you find dead people. Psychologically, they are ruining us. I don't know if that's what they want: for us to give in to despair and go home. They're mistaken. In my case, I won't let my guard down until I find my son and take him home. And I mean walking.

MOTHER OF ONE OF THE FORTY-THREE DISAP-PEARED STUDENTS DURING A PROTEST IN FRONT OF THE 27TH BATALLION ARMY BASE IN IGUALA, 18 DECEMBER 2014. Give us back our sons! That is our only demand. We want our sons alive. Just like you took them, that's how we want them back. Remember that you too have children. If your son were disappeared, what would you do? Would you be calm? Would your home be peaceful? Do you want us to get over this pain? How can you want us to go home if our homes are not calm, not peaceful? We are outraged because we don't know where our sons are. Give us back our sons! They're the ones who have them. The government has them. They're the ones who took them, who disappeared them. They're the ones holding them. We want our sons!

FROM AN ARGENTINE FORENSIC ANTHROPOLO-GY TEAM (EAAF) PRESS RELEASE DATED 7 DECEM-BER 2014, MEXICO CITY. During a press conference on October 31, 2014, the PGR [Mexican federal attorney general's office] shared testimony of arrested suspects indicating that they had burned the students' remains at the Cocula trash dump, placing in plastic bags the ash and bone fragments recovered from said remains.

According to those same testimonies, the suspects would have thrown the bags into the San Juan River in

Cocula. According to what the PGR told EAAF, federal police divers recovered the bone fragment in question from a plastic bag found in the San Juan River, which the federal police divers subsequently handed over to PGR investigators. The EAAF was not present at the moment the divers and investigators recovered said bag; the EAAF neither participated in nor witnessed the discovery of said fragment. The PGR called the EAAF to the location once the bag of remains was already open and the sample in question was already placed with other samples on a clean surface. The EAAF participated in other findings of remains on the shore of said river with PGR investigators.

The EAAF wishes to state that this does not affect the identification [of a sample] but considers that it is important to clarify that the EAAF was not witness to the discovery of the fragment that led to the indentification.

Lastly, it is the EAAF's opinion at this moment that there is not sufficient scientific certainty or physical evidence to conclude that the remains recovered from the San Juan River by PGR investigators, and in part by the EAAF, correspond to remains recovered from the Cocula trash dump in the manner described by the suspects. Burned and incinerated remains were recovered both from the San Juan River and the Cocula trash dump. The evidence that links the two locations is, for the moment, essentially testimonial; that is, for the moment it stems from the suspects' testimonies. In the EAAF's opinion, greater physical evidence joining the discoveries from both locations is needed and the examination of the remains as well as the search operations for the disappeared should continue.

FROM AN INTERVIEW WITH A MUNICIPAL EM-PLOYEE OF THE COCULA TRASH DUMP, 16 JUNE 2015.

"After that day, did you continue working at the trash dump?"

"Yes."

"And you didn't notice anything. . . ."

"No. Nothing, nothing."

". . . strange? A large fire, or. . . ."

"Nothing. Nothing at all."

"About what time was it when you all went to the dump?"

"It was around noon when we went to dump the trash."

"Did you notice anything strange?"

"No. In all truth we didn't notice anything."

"On the day of the twenty-seventh?"

"Yes, on the twenty-seventh."

"And there was nothing there?"

"No, there was nothing there."

"Had it rained that night?"

"It rained."

"Did it rain hard?"

"It rained more or less hard. It was coming down all night, so it was raining. It didn't stop until around six-thirty or seven in the morning."

FORMER MUNICIPAL EMPLOYEE OF THE COCULA TRASH DUMP, 16 JUNE 2015. We went up to the dump that day, September 27; it was our turn to work the weekend. Like normal, that day it was our turn to work the weekend. We also went to dump the trash there on Sunday the twenty-eighth. We went a bit later than normal because it had rained. It's just up that way. We got there, dumped the trash; that's the job we do. We got to the dump more or less around one in the afternoon. Around then. I think so, because we left around noon. So somewhere around one or two we got there. But we didn't see anything. Everything was normal. We didn't go earlier because when it rains the road can get muddy. And that's it: we got there, dumped the trash, and came back. The twenty-sixth we didn't go up there. Nor on the twenty-fifth. There's another trash dump over on this side in Apipilulco. But when it rains the road out there gets really bad and we can't get through. On Saturdays and Sundays the trash collection route goes through this area: the market, the *zócalo*, and San Miguel on Saturdays; on Sundays we pick up through the outlying neighborhood. We pick up the trash wherever, the *zócalo*, wherever. And then we go through the outlying neighborhood, and since it is closer, from there we head out toward the dump. It's on the way. When we pick up trash here in Cocula, sometimes we go and dump over here, because it's a bit closer. The truth is we went and dumped the trash and everything was normal. Green, green, everything the same as always. The same, normal. We just went to do our job: dump the trash. And we didn't see anything: not this, nor that. Normal.

But, well, they also want to give us a fright. So now we don't know anything. They came to get us. . . . The PGR came to give us a scare. That we don't know anything, that what the fuck, we didn't see anything. Really, who knows? We do our jobs, our work.

Honestly: I don't know anything, I didn't see anything.

"No, but did you work?"

Well, yes, we worked. We have to work. Not like we could leave our work just like that, I told him. Now it's over.

But. . . . It was on November 2. We went; they came for us. I was working.

"You all are going to give your testimony," they said.

"Well, I don't know anything," I said. "Take me wherever you want. Who owes nothing fears nothing." They wanted to scare us. Or, who knows? I really don't know. But, well, we went.

Well, honestly, I don't know how to read. And, well, once we got there they separated us: one over here, the other over there. And they said:

"Right now you both are going to Nayarit." It was something I never imagined. And, how to tell you, they held us there. We didn't see anything. And, how do they want us to say something if we didn't. . . ? They had us there without food. We went at around two in the afternoon.

We put down our fingerprints. They made us put our fingerprints and sign. What can I tell you? We signed so many pieces of paper that they made for us. I told them that I don't know how to read. I couldn't read it. I can barely scribble my name. And they made so many. . . . Honestly, I never in my life thought something like this would happen. They made us read I don't know what. And I, like I tell you, I told them right away that I don't know how to read. Why did they give me all that stuff? They put so many pieces of paper in front of me.

FROM THE INTERDISCIPLINARY INDEPENDENT EXPERT GROUP (GIEI) REPORT, PAGE 156. [The] expert analysis shows that there is no existing evidence to support the hypothesis posited in testimonies that forty-three bodies were cremated in the Cocula trash dump on September 27, 2014.

BLANCA NAVA VÉLEZ, MOTHER OF JORGE ÁLVAREZ NAVA, 19, FRESHMAN, DURING A PRESS CONFERENCE IN MEXICO CITY, 6 SEPTEMBER 2015. We mothers and fathers were right. We were always right! Our sons were not burned. That is the truth. We knew that what the government said was a lie. Another lie. And now we stand here to tell whoever framed all that, they were wrong. They couldn't deceive us. I said that to Murillo Karam: not even he believed his lies. And now we've shown it to them with proof. Not like him, with lies. We have scientific proof that our children are alive. And we are going to find them. The state is guilty. Because three levels of government participated. And who is going to guarantee to us that from here on they won't come out with another lie? Because we won't believe it. They couldn't deceive us with that lie, now even less so. We will continue pushing forward for our sons! We will keep fighting, and we will keep shouting. I told the government once, and I'll say it again: we are poor, but we're not stupid. We're not going to believe this. And a mother's heart can't be wrong. Our sons were not burned there! And we're proving it. I hope that from now on they only tell the truth. We don't want any more lies. As mothers and fathers here today: we want the truth. We don't want any more lies. We will not accept another lie from the government. Because the government has dedicated itself to torturing us, to destroying out hearts. Did they think that with that lie we didn't feel wretched? We said to him: don't you have children? And look what he did. And now we're showing him that the theatre he built has crumbled to ruins. His "historical truth" is a historical lie! And we will keep going until we find our children; we will fight until we find them!

MIGUEL ALCOCER, 20, FRESHMAN. I had nightmares. I dreamt that the police were shooting at us again and woke up afraid. I didn't even want to sleep. Once, I dreamt that I was in my house with my parents and some men arrived. At first they came up to us all friendly and cool, but I already felt something. I told my parents that the men were bad, but they said no they weren't. And one day we came home, me, my mom and dad, and my brothers, we came home and saw the man that my parents trusted. And I saw that he was cutting someone into pieces. I was fucking terrified and saw that my parents were also afraid. That day I felt like shit all day. I felt my whole body nervous, terrible. But nowadays I haven't dreamt like that.

EDGAR YAIR, 18, FRESHMAN. I feel sad because we had deep friendships with all my *compañeros* who are disappeared. More than friendship, we had a kind of brotherhood. Because we spent a lot of time together. We were together every day. We shared sadness, joy, laughter. Sometimes anger. I had a really deep friendship with a *compañero* who is disappeared. I didn't feel like he was a friend anymore, I felt like he was a brother. Now it hurts me that those *compañeros* can't be found.

JORGE HERNÁNDEZ ESPINOSA, 20, FRESHMAN. I want to graduate from the college and become a teacher. I want to tell my children and grandchildren one day that I studied in the Raúl Isidro Burgos Teachers College at Ayotzinapa. When I do, I will feel proud about saying that I was there during the massacre of September 26, when the whole country, the whole world heard the news and supported us. Some people criticized us, but everyone heard the news from Ayotzinapa about how we were attacked.

I am proud to say that I am part of the freshman class; I am an Ayotzinapa Teachers College student.

COYUCO BARRIENTOS, 21, FRESHMAN. There is a phrase that many people here say: Whoever sees an act of injustice and does not combat it, commits it.

AFTERWORD

BY THE FIRST DAYS OF OCTOBER 2014, the Ayotzinapa Rural Teachers College basketball court had become a kind of open-air waiting room of despair. Pain emanated like heat. Under the court's high, corrugated tin roof, 43 families gathered to face the hours between search expeditions, protests, and meetings with government officials, human rights workers, and forensic anthropologists. Gathered in clumps at the court's edges, sitting on the concrete floor or in plastic folding chairs formed in semicircles, they spoke in hushed tones and kept mostly to themselves. Most had traveled from small indigenous and *campesino* communities in Guerrero's mountainsides. Many had arrived without a change of clothes. They had all come to look for their sons.

News of the police attacks was initially met with muted outrage. Six people killed and dozens of students disappeared by the police in the middle of Iguala? It didn't seem possible. The first list of missing students had 57 names on it. Within a day or two many students had seen their names included among the disappeared and had called the school to let student organizers know that they were safe, that they had escaped from the shootings in Iguala that night and gone home rather than back to the school. The list quickly went from 57 to 43 names. Guerrero state officials told the press not to worry, that surely the other 43 students had also gone home, or were hiding in the hillsides and would be calling in soon. Never mind that the students were last seen being forced into the backs of municipal police trucks. Still, it wasn't until a week later, on October 4, 2014, when state prosecutors uncovered the first of a series of mass graves on the outskirts of Iguala, that the sense of disbelief eroded, and the national and international media descended on the region. When it became clear that the charred remains of 28 people found in those graves did not belong to any of the missing students, the core of collective anger began to crystallize. Mass marches took place in cities across the country. In Guerrero, Ayotzinapa students—with the 43 families looking on—smashed windows and set government buildings on fire. In Iguala, protesters sacked and burned the municipal palace.

Though it was neither an isolated event nor the largest killing or mass disappearance in recent years, something about the horror unleashed that night in Iguala removed the government's mask of repose. The scale of the violence: that police killed six, wounded more than 40, and disappeared 43 people. The theatrical cruelty: that they cut off a student's face. And then that those who suffered the attacks were mostly freshmen college students from one of the most combative colleges in the country. That the attackers were mostly uniformed police officers. That within days the mayor of Iguala, his wife, and the police chief—all suspects in the attacks—went into hiding. That when the state and federal governments finally started to search for the missing students they did so by looking in the ground. That the government so quickly then found mass graves, and that the remains found there were not those of the students. That the government treated the mothers and fathers searching for their sons with ineptitude and disregard.

Something about the events in Iguala—the combination of horror, state culpability, and well-crafted official incompetence—struck at the very core of a people exhausted by violence and government depravity. Anger was everywhere palpable. Outcry rose from nearly every sector of society. Something appeared to break. Mexico, in early November 2014, was a nation in pain. And all of the protests gave voice to one resolute demand: *Bring them back alive.*

By late September 2014, before the attacks, Mexico was supposed to be in the grip of its Moment. President Enrique Peña Nieto of the Institutional Revolutionary Party had overseen sweeping education and energy reforms and the arrest of Joaquín "El Chapo" Guzmán, Mexico's "most wanted" man (he would later escape, get arrested again, and then be extradited to the United States in January 2017). The gruesome images of murder that defined the administration of Felipe Calderón from the National Action Party (2006–2012) no longer dominated the daily newspapers. *Time* magazine put Peña Nieto on the cover of its February 2014 issue with the headline "Saving Mexico." The mid-September news of an army massacre in Tlatlaya, State of Mexico, led to scandal and the quick arrest of at least a few of the implicated soldiers, something that never occurred on Calderón's watch. From a distance, on the surface, it might have seemed that Mexico's long nightmare of violence was waning.

President Peña Nieto's inauguration on December 1, 2012, marked the return of the Institutional Revolutionary Party (PRI) after 12 years of National Action Party (PAN) rule. The PRI had governed Mexico from 1929 to 2000 without interruption. Presidents held one six-year term and then stepped off stage. The incoming president turned a blind eye to the previous administration's crimes and the outgoing president abandoned national political life. This system allowed Mexico's elite to overcome murderous infighting while constructing a state apparatus capable of silencing all opposition through bribery, electoral sleight-of-hand, and bloody repression. The president stood atop a pyramidal power structure in which every lower level reproduced the pyramid. Governors, for example, bowed to the president nationally, but ruled as mini-presidents in their states.

For decades the system withstood all challenges. In 1968, then-president Gustavo Díaz Ordaz used the army to repress the student movement, massacring hundreds during a protest in Tlatelolco Plaza in Mexico City on October 2. Thousands joined clandestine armed revolutionary movements following the massacre. The government sought to annihilate the guerrilla organizations using death squads, forced disappearances, and torture throughout the 1970s and 1980s. In 1988, opposition candidate Cuauhtémoc Cárdenas mounted a serious electoral challenge, and the PRI responded first with election fraud and later with a killing spree of members of the Democratic Revolutionary Party (PRD) that Cárdenas and others created after the elections. The PRI government sent the army and then paramilitary death squads to repress the Zapatista insurgency that began on January 1, 1994.

But the cumulative power of the challenges gained unprecedented momentum in the 1990s, and under such pressure the political pact dissolved. On March 23, 1994 one or maybe two gunmen shot the PRI's then–presidential candidate Luis Donaldo Colosio in the head, in public, on camera. By the end of the following administration (1994–2000) the PRI was thoroughly discredited and reviled. Vicente Fox of the conservative PAN won the election, breaking the PRI's 71-year reign. Fox's six-year term was marked by legislative stalemates, corruption scandals, and widespread protest. The 2006 elections became mired in allegations of fraud, and PAN candidate Felipe Calderón took office with the weakest mandate in Mexican history. He quickly militarized the country in a "war on drug traffickers." During his term more than 120,000 people were murdered and at least another 23,000 were reported "disappeared." Massacres and mutilated bodies displayed on roadsides became quotidian headlines. Federal and state prosecutors investigated a mere 2 to 5 percent of the murders. In 2008, Jorge Juárez Loera, the military commander in charge of Operation Chihuahua, told reporters: "Instead of saying another dead person, you should say one less criminal." Within a year, the main city under his command, Ciudad Juárez, would become the murder capital of the world.

Throughout the PRI's reign, Guerrero always ranked among the states most active in opposition movements and government repression. In the late 1960s and early '70s, Lucio Cabañas and Genaro Vázquez—both Ayotzinapa graduates—took arms in Guerrero following police repression of their social movements. The Mexican army killed and disappeared hundreds of people in an attempt to annihilate guerrilla movements in that era. In the late 1980s and early '90s, hundreds of grassroots PRD activists were killed in Guerrero. In the 1990s, state police massacred 17 *campesinos* and wounded 21 during a roadside ambush in Aguas Blancas. Then-governor Ruben Figueroa resigned amidst scandal after unedited police video footage of the massacre was leaked to the press.

Ángel Aguirre Rivero of the PRI stepped in as Governor Figueroa's replacement. While Aguirre was in office, the army massacred 11 people suspected of belonging to a guerrilla movement while they slept in a schoolhouse in the small indigenous community of El Charco. Aguirre, now with the PRD, won state elections in 2011 and took office again in April of that year. On December 12, 2011, Ayotzinapa students blocked the Mexico City–Acapulco federal highway in Chilpancingo to pressure Aguirre to increase the school's admissions quota and the daily food budget. Within minutes, plainclothes state police opened fire on the protest and killed two students: Jorge Alexis Herrera Pino and Gabriel Echeverría de Jesús. No one has been punished for the killings.

Every year 140 students come to the all-male the Raúl Isidro Burgos Rural Teachers College in Ayotzinapa from some of the most economically battered places in the hemisphere. They live on campus but pay no tuition or board. (While Ayotzinapa is an all-male college, other rural teachers colleges are all female, and others are coed.) The state government provides a meal budget that amounts to $3.70 per student per day (increased after the police killings in 2011), and hence a diet that seldom strays from eggs, rice, and beans. The first-year dorm rooms are windowless concrete boxes with no furniture, where students sleep as many as eight to a room, laying out cardboard and blankets for bedding. Some fasten empty plastic milk crates to the walls to use as dressers.

Though the buildings are in need of repair or reconstruction (a 2012 National Human Rights Commission report stated that many of the dwellings "violated the students' human rights" and "were not fit for habitation"), the most visually striking things at Ayotzinapa are the murals and stencil art. Buildings feature portraits of revolutionaries such as Lucio Cabañas and Genaro Vázquez, Subcomandante Marcos, and Che Guevara, and murals depicting mass mobilizations, indigenous resistance, and the 2011 police murder of Jorge Alexis Herrera and Gabriel Echeverría. The school grounds, which include fields of corn, beans, a few vegetables, and flowers are well kept without employees paid to do so. The students do all the farming, cleaning, tending, fixing, and painting, and a large part of the cooking. And like college students across the world, they are absorbed in the purpose and routines of their particular lives. Class time and homework make up the least of it. I rarely heard a student speak about their classes. (Students said that the state government intentionally hires teachers opposed to their social organizing.) Instead, the subjects of enthusiasm are most often student-organizing activities; sports, music, and dance clubs; classroom observations conducted in rural schools throughout the state; and just the place itself, Ayotzinapa. These are youth whom the political system tells they have no place. They are the ones apparently destined to enter the lowest ranks of the drug-warring armies or scramble across the Arizona desert and pick bell peppers in California or wash dishes in Chicago. Ayotzinapa offers them a different route, a profession: to become rural elementary school teachers. Ayotzinapa says to them, "You belong here."

Ayotzinapa is a Náhuatl word meaning a place of turtles, and there is something about luxury passenger buses that resembles turtles. One of the most common "activities," as the students call their organizing actions, is—for lack of a better word—commandeering buses. For Ayotzinapa students, their travels to observe teachers in rural areas are an essential—indeed, state-mandated—part of the curriculum. The college however, in early September 2014, had only two buses, two vans, a pickup truck, and no budget to rent or acquire new vehicles. The students, for many years, had found a way to secure transportation themselves: boarding a stopped bus—often achieved by first setting up a highway blockade—and informing its driver and passengers that the bus would be used for the educational purposes of the Ayotzinapa Teachers College.

In the immediate aftermath of the attacks in Iguala, government officials decried the students' tactics as wanton thievery. Both the police and the companies had tolerated the practice, if begrudgingly, for years. Moreover, the students are not thieves: they return the buses unharmed, and they "reach an agreement with the drivers." Such an agreement—for the bus drivers never abandon the vehicles, sometimes camping out at the college, with meals provided, for weeks or even months—involves compensation. The students pay the drivers after the "hijacking" (a term even the students sometimes use to describe their actions), hence the drivers "agree" to go along with it. I spoke to bus drivers who loathe the practice, others who feel indifferent to it—it's just another day of work—and others who enjoy it, saying that it gives them more time off, which they often use to visit family in nearby towns, asking the students to cover for them if the company calls.

The students, when they block highways, typically do so at tollbooths, or just before them. When they are able to take over a tollbooth, then the drivers coming through, relieved of their toll duties, might be inclined to "donate" that money to the students. Often, however, the students will block the road just before the tollbooth, asking for donations independently of the tolls. None of these tactics are unique to Ayotzinapa students, but by 2014 they had become fully integrated into the basic functioning of the school.

The government's accusations against the students do not stop, though, at calling them bus thieves. For years, government officials have accused Ayotzinapa of being a kind of nursery for armed movements. In May 2013, Televisa reporter Adela Micha interviewed Governor Ángel Aguirre on her program. She asked him how it was possible that the Ayotzinapa students had made a "habitual" practice of "stealing" buses. Aguirre responded that Ayotzinapa, "has become a kind of bunker. Neither the federal nor the state governments can access the school. It is a place that has been used by some groups to indoctrinate these youths and cultivate social resentment amongst them." Micha then asked him: "Who is indoctrinating them?" Aguirre responded: "A few insomniac guerrillas."

"Governor Aguirre said that the students had taken control of the school and that no one could get in: it was a way of saying that the school was lawless, a no-man's-land. But the truth is that the governor himself visited the school in 2011. He was in the dining hall when he made a public commitment to provide the support that the students asked for," said Kau Sirenio in early October 2014. Sirenio, a friend I have known for several years, is an indigenous Ñuu Savi journalist from the Costa Chica region of Guerrero. He writes for the Chilpancingo-based weekly *Trinchera*, hosts a bilingual weekly radio program in Spanish and Tu'un Savi, and has covered Ayotzinapa since 2004. "That day in 2011," Sirenio told me, "the students tried to get Aguirre to sign an agreement, but he said that he would do so two weeks later, at the governor's office. Two weeks later he postponed the meeting. He then kept putting off the meeting. In November, the students started going to the local radio stations to demand that the governor sign the commitment. Then came December. The students couldn't wait any longer because they were trying to negotiate the school's budget for 2012. They wanted to increase the incoming class from 140 to 160 students. They also wanted to increase the daily food budget from 20 pesos to 60 pesos per student per day. [In 2011 the peso was worth about

0.07 dollars.] But Aguirre didn't sign the commitment, and so the students blocked the federal highway on December 12. That is when the police killed Jorge Alexis Herrera Pino and Gabriel Echeverría de Jesús. And still, after the repression that day, the state government unleashed a kind of dirty war smear campaign against Ayotzinapa, saying that they had no reason to block the highway. In January 2012, the government organized a march to support the governor and demand the closing of Ayotzinapa. That is when they really began demonizing the students. What happened in Iguala was the fruit of that hate campaign of 2012 and the impunity in the case of the two murdered students in 2011. Because they showed in 2011 that in Guerrero the murderers of students are not punished."

The plan for September 26, 2014, never involved going to Iguala. The students had no idea that the mayor and his wife would be hosting an event that evening in the town's central plaza. Most of them did not know who the mayor of Iguala was. The plan, rather, was to try and grab some buses in Chilpancingo and, if that didn't work, to take two buses of first-year students out to Huitzuco—some 20 miles from Iguala—slow down cars on the highway, collect donations, and hope a bus would appear in the traffic.

In mid-September, representatives of the Federation of Socialist *Campesino* Students of Mexico (FECSM) from rural teachers colleges across the country gathered for an annual assembly in Amilcingo, State of Mexico. The assemblies are usually held in June, but had been postponed until September that year. Among other affairs, the student representatives voted on which college would host delegations from the other colleges prior to traveling to Mexico City to participate in the annual October 2 march commemorating the 1968 student massacre in the capital's Tlatelolco plaza.

That day, September 16, 2014, the FECSM representatives from across Mexico chose Ayotzinapa, even though it wasn't supposed to be their turn that year. Another school said they couldn't host, Ayotzinapa volunteered, and the assembly approved. Hundreds of students from the 15 other rural teachers colleges across the country would thus all gather at Ayotzinapa and from there travel as a caravan to Mexico City to take to the streets 46 years after the Mexican army gunned students down in those very same streets in the lead-up to the 1968 Olympics. As host, then, Ayotzinapa would have to provide food and transportation for the caravan. That meant getting buses. A lot of buses.

This is worth keeping in mind: the rural college students, most of them freshmen, who went out to commandeer buses on the evening of September 26, 2014, most of them doing so for the first time, were trying to commandeer those buses to attend the annual protest of one of the worst student massacres in history.

Over the course of that Saturday, September 27, 2014, state forces arrested 22 Iguala police officers. The surviving students identified those police officers, which means they were only the ones that they could see shooting at them from the front and the sides of the buses, and not the ones wearing face masks who disappeared their classmates from the third bus on Álvarez Street, nor the police who attacked the fourth bus in front of the state courthouse, nor the state or federal police who also participated in the coordinated attacks.

Families of Ayotzinapa students arrived at the school that Saturday from all over hoping to find their sons. On Monday, September 29, Mayor José Luis Abarca gave an interview to Chilpancingo-based journalist Sergio Ocampo. Ocampo asked him for "his version" of what happened.

Ocampo shared his recording of the interview with me. Abarca said that he had been working up a sweat dancing after the DIF event and then went with his wife and daughters to a restaurant. While dining, he said that he got a call from Felipe Flores Velázquez, the Iguala police chief, telling him that "the Ayotzinapa students were involved in some disturbances, that they had taken some buses from the station. So, I indicated that he should let them be . . . that I don't want any . . . assault, um, eh, problem with them. Because we know in advance that they enjoy, um, well, riling people. So I gave instructions for the forces to keep their distance, that I didn't want any problems."

The following day, Mayor Abarca and his wife, María de los Ángeles Pineda Villa, went into hiding. President Peña Nieto canceled a previously scheduled trip to Guerrero, citing unfavorable weather conditions. (He did not, however, cancel his early November trip to China and Australia. To this day he has not set foot in Ayotzinapa or the scenes of the multiple attacks in Iguala. He has, however, urged people to "get over" the killings and disappearances.)

The initial search efforts that week involved state police driving groups of parents around Iguala, occasionally stopping to suggest that they, the parents, knock on a given door and ask if their children were hiding there. Nardo Flores Vázquez, father of Bernardo Flores Alcaráz, told me in March 2015 that he had traveled to Iguala the day after the attacks with two other parents from his hometown in the Costa Grande region of Guerrero. They went to the city jail, to the morgue, and to the army base without luck, before heading to Ayotzinapa and joining the other families there.

"The government didn't give us any information," he said, "only that the boys were disappeared and that the government would look for them. We went with the government to look for them in Iguala and on the outskirts of town. And then the following week we went searching for them with the Marines through the hillsides, but I didn't trust in the government's search efforts from the beginning. I could tell they were just going through the motions, making a pantomime of looking for the students."

Then, on Saturday, October 4, the Guerrero state prosecutor announced the discovery of four mass graves in the hills outside of Iguala. An initial excavation revealed an unknown number of charred human remains. The architects of this killing had placed logs under the people before dousing them in diesel fuel and setting them on fire in the ditches. According to an officer I questioned there that afternoon, information from a person being tortured led them to the site. "They squeezed one of those guys and he sang," the police said.

Governor Aguirre, amidst calls for his resignation, gave a press conference that evening committing himself and his government to searching for the students, and then invited the families to speak with him privately. Plainclothes police ushered the mothers and fathers, aunts and uncles, brothers and sisters through metal detectors before leading them into the room with Aguirre. Mario Contreras, a short, wiry 49-year-old tinsmith, stood before the governor without extending his hand.

"Good evening," Aguirre said, smiling. His greeting met silence.

"Yes?" the governor added, "Tell me."

"What do you want me to tell you? Good evening? For you. For us with our guts tied in knots, with our guts a fucking wreck. . . . Our only fucking crime is being too poor to send our kids to a private school. Lucky it's not your son.

They'd find your son in less than half an hour, you asshole, and without a fucking scratch."

Contreras and Aguirre faced each other there across a fissure, which their brief conversation became a doomed attempt to bridge. The rupture between them, signaling class tensions and power disparities, also revealed a pain differential: Aguirre, the governor, was seeking to save his political career, and Contreras, the tinsmith, his son.

"You do not know the pain we feel," Contreras told him. The fissure would expand in the coming days and weeks, with growing calls for the students to be found alive and their attackers brought to justice on one side, and speculation about temperatures at which bones disintegrate in a diesel-fed fire during a rainstorm on the other.

Contreras had last spoken to his son César on the telephone around 3:00 p.m. on Friday, September 26, 2014. Contreras was then recovering from typhoid fever, and his son had called to check up on him. Upon hearing his father's voice, César said that he wanted to ask for permission to take leave for the weekend and make the 10-hour trip back to his hometown in the state of Tlaxcala to help take care of his father. But the school year had just begun and Contreras didn't want his son to be distracted. He told him to stay put.

"That was the worst mistake of my life, a mistake I cannot forgive myself for," Contreras told me. "But I told him: 'You know what, I sent you off to study.'"

The next morning Contreras saw the headlines: six people killed and, at that time, 57 students disappeared. He and his wife, Hilda Hernández, got a ride from a friend, driving the 10 hours to Ayotzinapa and arriving around 1:30 a.m. that Sunday to find their son's name and image amongst the 43 thumb-size black-and-white photographs making up the revised list of the disappeared. From that moment on,

Mario Contreras and Hilda Hernández—like the men and women of the 42 other families—slept on the bare floors of classrooms, ate what students and neighbors handed them, changed into donated clothing, and spent countless hours between protests and meetings gathered around the shaded edges of the Ayotzinapa basketball court.

The Mexican federal government soon took over the investigation but continued to look for, and find, mass graves and incinerated human remains. The parents of the 43 disappeared students wanted their children, not bones and ash. They called on the government to reorient its search and began a series of fierce protests demanding that the government return their sons and classmates alive.

"They are leading us in circles," Contreras told me in early October, during a large march in Chilpancingo that shut down the federal highway connecting Mexico City and Acapulco for hours. "They're telling us there are ten dead bodies in Taxco, there are twelve dead bodies over there. Now they've found mass graves. So now they're going to give us those bodies, all charred and foul? I say, no sir. You all took them alive and you have to bring them back alive. It wasn't some criminal organization that took them, and we're supposed to think they've already been killed. It was the police who took them!"

Parents and students blocked federal highways, marched through cities, smashed the windows of the Guerrero state congress and the governor's offices and set them on fire. During all these protests, police were nowhere to be seen. Soon people across Mexico and the world took to the streets, the airwaves, and cyberspace to support the families. Shortly after the second round of national mobilizations, Governor Aguirre resigned. On October 29, the parents met with President Enrique Peña Nieto and his cabinet.

The families told him that if he was incapable of finding their children alive, he should follow Aguirre's example and step aside. (Recall that Aguirre was first appointed interim governor after Rubén Figueroa was forced to resign following the masscare of Aguas Blancas: the cyclical patterns of horror repeat under the reign of impunity.)

On November 4, 2014, federal authorities arrested Abarca and Pineda in Mexico City, and shortly after, on November 7, the then–attorney general Jesús Murillo Karam announced that on the night of the attack, police delivered the students to a drug gang who then murdered and incinerated them in an open-air trash dump in Cocula, about 15 miles from Iguala. (He did not mention the rainstorm that lasted all night.) The supposed killers, according to Murillo Karam, then scooped up the human ash, deposited it into plastic bags, took those plastic bags to a nearby shallow river, emptied six bags into the river, and then threw in the last two bags unopened. After leading reporters through a series of supposed confessions, Murillo Karam cut short a reporter's question and the press conference itself by saying, "*Ya me cansé*"—Now I'm tired. His words soon became the subject of viral social media mockery. The government announced that it would send the charred bone pieces recovered from a trash bag supposedly found on the bank of a river near the trash dump to a specialized DNA laboratory at the University of Innsbruck in Austria. The parents rejected the federal prosecutor's claims and initiated a new round of heated protests, including more property destruction targeting Guerrero state government buildings. They then set out in three caravans traveling across the country to call for support. On November 20, 2014, the 104th anniversary of the Mexican Revolution, the three caravans reconvened in Mexico City and led many tens of thousands of people marching from three locations, eventually funneling into Reforma Avenue and the *Zócalo*, the central plaza and symbolic civil core of the nation.

In the days both leading up to and following that march, Mexico City seemed to pulse with solidarity for the disappeared students. Newspaper front-pages, conversations, graffiti and stencil art, everywhere one turned, Ayotzinapa was there. Walk through the hip Roma neighborhood and you would see an unattended altar of candles and poster-board signs near the fountain in the Rio de Janeiro Park demanding justice for the 43. Walk through the working-class Obrera neighborhood and you would see a large window-less wall with five-foot-tall red block letters painted over a white background declaring, *"Ayotzinapa: Fue el Estado"*— Ayotzinapa: It Was the State. The sports tabloid *Record* ran a blacked-out front page with the headline: "#INDIGNA-TION: Mexico has had enough. Mexico is in mourning."

Early one Sunday, some 700 athletes organized an impromptu race down the length of Reforma Avenue, all runners wearing the number 043. During the multi-Grammy-winning band Calle 13's concert at the Palacio de Deportes, some 15,000 people periodically counted in unison to 43 then shouted: *"¡Justicia!"* Tom Morello, of Rage Against the Machine fame, dedicated a guest guitar solo to Ayotzinapa, flipping his guitar around to play with his teeth, and revealing the number 43 taped to the back of the guitar. During the show, the band invited a group of parents and students from Ayotzinapa on stage to speak. One of the parents was Mario Contreras.

"Good evening," he said, "I am the father of César Manuel González Hernández. My apologies: I am not a public speaker, nor any kind of leader. I am nothing more than a wounded father from whom they are trying to tear away the most beautiful thing life has given me: my son, whom I love and want to come home along with his 42 classmates."

But the solidarity also seemed to contain an element of fear. If the police *are* the drug gangs, and the state and federal authorities can or will only search for missing people in shallow graves and discarded trash bags, and all three major political parties are implicated in massacres of this scale, then what is to be done? The horror unleashed in Iguala stripped away the façade of a Mexican Moment led by Peña Nieto and the PRI, and created a widespread call for fundamental political change, while at the same time thrashing whatever hope remained of achieving such change through existing institutions and the electoral process.

One of the Ayotzinapa caravans traveled to Oventik in Zapatista territory on November 15. Through their spokesperson, Subcomandante Insurgente Moisés, the Zapatistas thanked them:

"Perhaps they have not told you, but it has been all of you, the families and *compañeros* of the murdered and disappeared students, who have been able, with the strength of your pain, with this pain turned into a dignified, noble rage, to lead many people in Mexico and the world to awaken, to question, to debate. For this we thank you." They also shared what their vision of change looks like: "We think that the moments that will change the world are not born in the calendars of the powerful, but are forged through the daily work, stubborn and continuous, of those who choose to organize themselves instead of joining the fashions of the day. There will be profound change, real transformations in this and other wounded lands." But such transformations, he said, "will not involve a change of administration but rather a change in the social relations, where the people govern, and the government obeys."

In the absence of an immediate institutional path in Mexico, there does seem to be, uncertain and shaky, a coming together of many paths of people to give the support that the state will not, or cannot, provide. One of the signs I saw in the November 20 march in Mexico City, handwritten on posterboard, read: "We do not know each other, but we need each other." By December, the Ayotzinapa basketball court had itself been transformed. One end of the court was filled with boxes upon boxes of donated food—canned tuna, rice, cooking oil, pasta, peppers, salsa—as well as clothing, medicine and books. Strung between the columns holding up the high tin roof were scores of photographs of protests and solidarity actions in cities across Mexico and the world. Families from the nearby towns of Tixtla and Zumpango del Río had set up buffet stations on folding tables with home-cooked meals available around the clock. In the space of a month the piercing absence of 43 students had been joined, for the time being, by the presence of many.

They call themselves the Other Disappeared, *Los otros desaparecidos*. They are the mothers and fathers, the brothers and sisters of men and women who were taken away in or near Iguala during the years and days before the attacks against the students, and never seen again. In many cases, witnesses identified police, soldiers, or "armed men" as assailants. The families of these disappeared had either been too afraid to speak out publicly or had slipped into desperation upon authorities' refusal to look for their loved ones. After police and unidentified gunmen killed six people and disappeared 43 Ayotzinapa students on the night of September 26–27 in Iguala, and after Guerrero state officials revealed mass graves containing 28 bodies that turned out not to be the students, the families of the "other disappeared" men and women decided to go out looking for their missing loved ones on their own, and underground.

Starting in November 2014, the group gathered every Sunday at the San Gerardo church with machetes, shovels, and iron rods and headed out into the sun-scorched hills surrounding Iguala looking for signs of shallow graves: recently turned earth, spots with a different color of soil, dips in the ground, anomalous articles of trash. When they found a place with one or more of these characteristics, they hammered a pointed iron rod a few feet into the dirt, pulled it back up, and smelled the tip. During one of these trials in February 2015, I too smelled the rod's point. "Slowly," they cautioned me. It was as unmistakable as it was assaulting: the smell of death.

In the first seven months of looking they found more than 100 bodies in places where state and federal investigators had supposedly searched and found none. They identified dozens more possible grave sites that still await excavation by federal investigators. And, as I write these words, every Sunday they head out again. Mayra and Mario Vergara, sister and brother, have spent every day since mid-November 2014 looking for the body of their brother, Tomás. During the week they divide their time between accompanying the federal authorities out to the sites they and other volunteers have identified, and scouting new locations based on anonymous tips. On Sundays they lead the group of family members looking for their sons and brothers, daughters and sisters, back out to fully comb areas they previously scouted. They call each of the human remains discovered "Tomás" until investigators are able to identify the bodies using DNA analysis.

Mayra, 37, and Mario, 42, grew up in Huitzuco. They have another sister who is a professor. Their father was murdered in a street fight 20 years ago. Their mother, Mario says, "cannot accept Tomás's disappearance, my mom is dying in life." Mario and Tomás began to work full time after their father's murder. Mario runs a small pool hall, and Tomás drove a taxi. On Thursday, July 5, 2012, the family gathered to celebrate Mayra's birthday, but Tomás didn't show up. Around ten o'clock that night someone called to say that Tomás had been kidnapped. That was when they started looking for him. They called other taxi drivers. They called the hospital where their grandfather had been recently admitted; Tomás had last been there sometime between 10 and 11 in the morning. That was the last time anyone saw him. They couldn't sleep that night. The following morning someone came to tell them that they had seen Tomás's taxi on the outskirts of town. Mayra went to the location and found that Tomás's cell phone, his wallet, the coins he used for change were all there in the taxi. There was no sign of violence. Later that day they got another call:

"I saw that you went to get his car. Do you believe this is a kidnapping now?" They asked for 300,000 pesos, then about 23,000 dollars. They said that if the family contacted the authorities they would kill Tomás. One of the family's uncles in Mexico City, however, said that the family should contact the federal anti-kidnapping unit.

"It was a civil war here in our house," Mario told me, "whether to call the police or not. I can't remember who convinced us to make the call or how we finally decided." The next morning they contacted the federal anti-kidnapping unit, which was then part of a federal organized crime investigative task force known as the SIEDO, and by the afternoon they had two agents in their house. The agents worked with the family on what they considered to be the fundamentals of kidnapping negotiations: always ask for proof of life, negotiate a lower ransom payment, and never make a full payment quickly. These were matters of "business" the agents said, and one must follow the rules of brokering tough business deals. When the kidnappers called, Mario asked for the "proof of life" only to hear the kidnappers unleash torrents of foul abuse:

"Bitch, we make the rules, we're in charge, we give the orders, shut the fuck up!"

Meanwhile the agents claimed to be tracking the calls.

"Every time there was a call," Mario said, "the agents told me that they were sending information to Mexico City so they could trace the call from there. We never saw any results from those investigations. Maybe they exist, maybe they don't, but we never saw anything." The agents continued to hold daily "training" sessions with Mario, pretending to be the kidnappers.

"They are here training you, and training you, and meanwhile your family member is on the other side," Mario said. The kidnappers asked for 300,000 pesos and Mario, following the coaching of the federal agents, offered $50,000. The kidnappers berated him:

"You have a pool hall, you fucker!" To which Mario would say:

"I'll sign it over to you, take it."

"Sell it, you piece of shit, and give us the money!"

"The tables are all old, no one is going to buy it quickly. Take it, I'll sign it over."

"You have cars! We've seen that you have a ton of cars!"

"Take them. They're all old."

The family was working hard to put together the 300,000 pesos, but the federal agents told them: "If you pay them the 300,000 quickly, they're just going to want more." Two months went by like that. Finally they reached an agreement to pay 80,000 pesos. It was a Saturday afternoon when the kidnappers called and said: "You know what, asshole? Time's up. Have the money ready tomorrow and it's done. We'll give you orders tomorrow."

The next day, Sunday, the kidnappers called and told Mario to be at the Corralón de Bandera in a certain number of minutes. "That was another problem with the agents," Mario said. "They didn't want anyone from the family to go make the payment. In moments like that you freeze up, you don't know what to do." The family scrambled to find someone to make the payment who was not a direct relative, who was trustworthy, who would take the risk, and whom the federal agents would accept. The kidnappers called back, leveling insults and threats. Mario, upon the agents' insistence asked again for the proof of life and, after another barrage of insult and threats the kidnappers said, "Okay, here's your brother."

"Bro, they kidnapped me, pull together from our friends whatever they ask." The kidnappers came on the line again:

"Did you hear him? Now come pay! I'll wait ten minutes!"

"When we heard that voice," Mario said, "no, our nerves, everyone, my mom, my sisters, everyone was crying. And the agents said: 'No, you can't go make the payment unless you are sure it is your brother.' It sounded like him, but we were all so nervous. The agents were recording all the calls. They played that part of the call back and said: 'Wait, wait, you have to be entirely sure that this is your brother. This is all business. Even if they get pissed, you have to wait for them to call again.'" The ten minutes passed. Another call came in.

"You son of a bitch! I'm going to kill him right now! And then I'm going to go and shoot every fucking one of you!

You fuckers!" Mario, pressured by the federal agents, asked again for the proof of life. "Do you think we're playing?" the kidnappers asked and then hung up. The agents said:

"This is a business, just wait. This is how it goes. We have a lot of experience with this." Maybe they had experience, and "it was their job," Mario told me, "but it was our brother."

A few minutes went by and the kidnappers called back. Again the insults and threats over the phone, the insistence from the federal agents on demanding proof of life, and Mario stuck in the middle, begging, pleading. Finally the kidnappers said they would hand the phone again to Tomás:

"Bro, they kidnapped me, pull together from our friends whatever they ask."

"You heard," they said, "be there in five minutes!"

The agents again had recorded the call and again they played it back: the same words, the same length of time. The agents said that it wasn't possible, it couldn't be Tomás, those were the same exact words, it had to be a recording.

"The time they gave us passed," Mario told me. "They called back. We had the speakerphone on. The last words they said were that we would regret this for the rest of our lives, that we would never know what happened to my brother."

In Iguala alone, a city of less than 150,000 residents, federal authorities received more than 250 reports of forced disappearance in less than a year after the attacks against the students. A Mexican Justice Department official told me that the bodies found by volunteers all came from an area of only two acres. Volunteers had by February 2015, marked 30 other possible shallow and mass graves in an area spanning more than 20 acres, he said.

I accompanied the Other Disappeared group on one of their Sunday expeditions. On a cloudless late February day in 2015, the temperature reached 39 degrees Celsius (102 degrees Fahrenheit). Some thirty volunteers spanned out across a steep, hillside cornfield. The stalks and husks of the last harvest lay sun-bleached and brittle on the ground. Federal police with assault rifles accompanied the group and stood guard around the perimeter of the field. Men and women ranging in age from their early twenties to their late seventies, dressed in long-sleeved shirts, hats, and bandannas covering their necks roamed in groups scanning the ground for hidden grave site characteristics. Mayra told me about her brother Tomás for the first time that day, and their decision to look for him in the hills and fields surrounding Iguala.

"Do you really think that after seeing all this cruelty," Mayra said, referring to the police attacks against the Ayotzinapa students and the 28 bodies pulled semi-charred from the hills on the edge of town "that my brother is still alive? The hope of finding him alive, once you've seen all these mass graves, that hope vanishes."

Mayra began to attend the very first marches and protests in Iguala after the attacks against the students. She made a banner asking if there would only be justice for mass disappearances. A few reporters approached her and she told them:

"If you only knew, there are not only 43 people disappeared, there are so many mothers looking for their children." Mayra was one of only a handful of people who went to the first meeting of families looking for their loved ones at the San Gerardo church in Iguala. By the time they held the second meeting in mid November, after the 28 bodies had been found, more than 100 people attended. They organized amongst themselves to start looking for more hidden mass graves in the hills.

Mayra said that the families of the Other Disappeared do not seek justice. They do not want to find the people who did these things to their children, to their siblings. They know that most of those people still roam free, and many wear police or military uniforms. They just want to find the remains of their loved ones, she said. This distinguishes them from so many others who have organized to pressure the government to look for the disappeared. Their slogan is: "Child, until I bury you, I won't stop looking."

Listening to the stories of the families looking for their loved ones in the hillsides near Iguala, I heard time and again testimonies describing how uniformed police officers participated in the disappearances. The police themselves controlled and administered kidnappings and sex trafficking in the region. One member of the Other Disappeared told me, "Abarca came in and put his police checkpoints around town, and a lot of people were disappeared as they tried to pass through those checkpoints."

In early October 2014, I spoke with an Iguala journalist who also survived the police attacks of September 26–27, 2014. He described the local police–organized crime structure that existed before the attacks this way: "The municipal police are the façade, but only a façade. They are not municipal police. They are narcos who use police uniforms, police weapons, and police vehicles. They call them *los bélicos* [the belligerents]. *Los bélicos* are police inside the municipal police who have a cartel. They are the ones who control the heavy stuff. The top guys. [. . .] There are about 300 *bélicos*, almost the entire police force. The cops who aren't in the cartel are a minority." He also told me: "The people who ordered and really carried out all that shit [on September 26–27, 2014] have not been arrested."

"The famous *bélicos*. They were police with official squad cars and everything, but they operated at night wearing face masks," Marina Hernández de la Garza, then an Iguala city councilwoman with the PRI, told me in Iguala in early October 2014. "If there were 400 police on the force, 300 of them were in the mafia. The cops that had the old banged-up trucks, those were the chumps. And the ones with the new, top-notch trucks, those were the mafia. When they came to deliver the new police trucks here, we said: look, those are the ones who will soon be robbing us." Hernández de la Garza said that the *bélicos* "would pick people up off the streets and give them an hour to turn over 10,000 pesos, or else. . . ."

In Mexico, police and military at every level have fully merged with forces of organized crime. It is no longer accurate to speak about corruption—if it ever was. Individuals who work inside and out of police and military forces carry out a wide range of violent acts inside a single network that combines both repressive and mercantile functions. The attacks on the streets of Iguala on September 26 and 27 exposed the evolving practices of the larger drug war machine, combining multiple forms of violence—murder, torture, mutilation, and forced disappearance—as acts of state terror and acts of business.

The U.S.-designed and -imposed drug war has enabled the growth and expansion of illegal markets in all areas of Mexican society, areas of state jurisdiction, and especially, areas of life and death. Terror has become a central feature not only of repression, but also of this market expansion. Gloria Arenas, a former guerrilla fighter and ex–political prisoner, told me in January 2015, while reflecting on the police–organized crime control of territory in her home state of Veracruz: "*Es que ya sin terror no hay negocio*" or, literally: "There is no business anymore without terror." Thus forced disappearance—a practice of state terror cultivated over decades to repress both armed insurgencies and unarmed social movements—has been taken up by the entrepreneurs of kidnapping and extortion.

Iguala is only one example of the terror zones created by the drug war in Mexico where families are condemned to live in fear and grief, scouring dry hillsides to look for the remains of their loved ones, people taken as commodities in the drug war's death markets and disappeared. The experiences of the Other Disappeared further reveal the daily, normalized realms of terror that existed before the violence unleashed against the students of Ayotzinapa.

Fear, terror, and horror are essential elements of both the illicit drug markets and the death markets that have expanded along with the constant fueling of the drug war itself. Just as illegality is part of the commodity form of substances like cocaine, heroin and marijuana, terror and horror have become parts of the commodity forms of mercantile killing: the reconfigured kidnapping, extortion, forced labor, human smuggling and human trafficking industries in Mexico.[10]

On December 7, 2014, the DNA lab at the University of Innsbruck, Austria, notified the Mexican government that

---

10. I have explored this analysis in "Without Terror, There Is No Business," *NACLA Report on the Americas*, Vol. 48, No. 2, Summer 2016, pp. 135–138, and "Las economías del terror," in Jorge Regalado, ed., *Pensamiento crítico, cosmovisiones, y epistemologías otras para enfrentar la guerra capitalista y construir autonomía*, Gualalajara: Universidad de Guadalajara-CIESAS-Jorge Alsonso, 2017, pp. 125–157. My analysis has been greatly influenced by Achille Mbembe's essay "Necropolitics" (2003, *Public Culture* 15 [1]: pp. 11–40).

it had identified one of the bone fragments as belonging to Alexander Mora Venancio, a 19-year-old Ayotzinapa student who was disappeared in Iguala. The government said that this identification amounted to "scientific proof" that the students had been burned in the Cocula trash dump. The Argentine Team of Forensic Anthropologists (EAAF)—one of the world's leading forensic anthropology organizations specializing in forced disappearances—had been representing the families alongside the federal investigators from the beginning of the Cocula trash dump investigation. The EAAF put out a communiqué on December 7 that stated: "At the moment there is not enough scientific certainty or physical evidence to claim that the remains recovered at the San Juan River by authorities . . . correspond to those removed from the Cocula trash dump in the manner indicated by the accused." The Argentine forensic anthropologists repeatedly emphasized that they were not present when the remains were supposedly pulled from the river, and that they had requested multiple times but never seen the official chain of custody documents corresponding to the discovery, removal, and initial treatment of those remains.

On January 26, 2015, the families and students held their monthly march in Mexico City. Once in the *Zócalo*, Carmen Cruz, mother of Jorge Aníbal Cruz Mendoza, said to the thousands of people gathered there:

"Good evening four months into this nightmare that we are living. These have been four months of pain, four months of suffering. We have wept, but not because our sons are dead. We have wept because we miss them. And I want to tell you that we have no doubt that government people have our sons. Because uniformed officials were the ones who took them, people following orders from a high command. Enrique Peña Nieto needs to stop playing the fool: even if he doesn't have them, he knows where they are. Give them back to us now. Every day we are thinking about where our sons could be. And once again we take to the streets to protest, demanding answers about where they are. With all of your support we will succeed. And I want to tell my son wherever he may be, don't think that I'm not looking for you. I am looking for you and I will find you."

Hilda Hernández Rivera, mother of César Manuel González Hernández said:

"The government has deceived us with so many lies. Unfortunately, we have come here to learn about all their bullshit. Forgive me if I speak with bad words. It makes me furious the kind of government we have, and that they try to deceive us, thinking we are stupid. We know what they are trying to do. And we will not permit it. My son is such a kind, kind person and I know that he knows his father and I are looking for him. And we will not stop looking. Yes, there are times when I cry, because it hurts, because he is my son. But it also makes me so angry, and that is what leads me to speak out now. I have not spoken out before. I have kept quiet, because I don't know what to say sometimes, but now I will say: we are not going to stand back with our arms crossed for our children. They have to reappear, because as a *compañero* just said, it was the police that took them, federal police and the army also participated. And there is nothing else to do but look for them. There is no one else, no drug traffickers or anything like that. Because here the drug traffickers are the government."

The following day, January 27, 2015, the Mexican federal attorney general, Jesús Murillo Karam, announced what he labeled "the historical truth" of the events in Iguala, which he had previously sketched in his November press conference, based on three testimonies (of men who would later denounce having been tortured into signing their confessions) claiming that the Iguala police, acting alone, had "turned the 43 students over" to gang members who took them out to an isolated trash dump near Cocula, murdered them and proceeded to incinerate their bodies from the predawn hours until 5:00 p.m. that Saturday afternoon with a fire built in the open air of wood and old tires.

The families were outraged. They held a press conference that same day. Cristina Bautista Salvador, mother of Benjamín Ascencio Bautista, said:

"We will not accept that our sons have already been killed. Just like they took them alive, we want them back alive. That is what we demand, and we will continue our struggle and our protests until they give us back our sons. Because out of a hundred people, 95 percent support us. And the 5 percent that is against us, that says we're just pestering, I assure them that if it were one of their children or grandchildren they would be here with us. And they would also be crying, like us. We are not crying because we feel like our sons are already dead, but because we miss them. We miss their voices, the way a son hugs, that's what's happening. We are in despair, that's why we cry. So we are not going to accept the government's refusal to return our sons. Officials have said that our sons are dead, but there is no proof."

Epifanio Álvarez Carvajal, father of Jorge Álvarez Nava, said:

"We would like to say, as parents, that the government has stepped all over our dignity. They have destroyed us. We do not accept what they are doing. First they told us that our sons were in the mass graves. And then, after that, they said in Cocula, in the trash dump. And now we can't be certain of anything. We can't accept anything they say, because there is not enough evidence to support it. So we as parents will keep struggling to find our sons, however we may find them, but we will fight to the end. This must be cleared up. That is why we as parents will not stop fighting. We can't go back to our homes with this pain."

The federal government's description of the coordinated attacks that night makes no mention of either state or federal police participating in the violence. The government's unproven claim that the police "turned the students over" to "narcos" is integral to the deliberate fabrication that the police and the narcos are distinct entities. To this day, the government's investigation fails to account for, or even address, state and federal police complicity in the atrocity, much less the role of the army.

In February 2015, the families of the disappeared students, the Mexican government, and the Inter-American Commission on Human Rights signed an agreement to establish an independent group of experts to conduct a parallel, though entirely independent, investigation. The group of five experts known in Mexico as the GIEI (Grupo Interdisciplinario de Expertos Independientes) was granted unprecedented access to the Mexican federal government's investigation. The experts nominated and accepted by all parties were Francisco Cox from Chile, Ángela Buitrago and Alejandro Valencia from Colombia, Claudia Paz y Paz Bailey from Guatemala, and Carlos Beristain from Spain. They arrived in Mexico for their initial six-month period in March 2015.

After a round of formal meetings with various Mexican federal agencies, the five experts went to meet with the families and the students in Ayotzinapa. When I had the opportunity to ask Cox and Beristain, at the end of their time in Mexico, which moments had most impacted them, they both, separately, referred to this first meeting.

"Something that hit us hard, really hard," Francisco Cox told me, "was when the families told us, 'You are our last hope, you have our trust.' But then what hit us, so intensely, was when they said, '*Por favor, no se vendan*' [please, don't sell out]. At first, I thought it was kind of offensive for someone to tell you 'don't sell out,' because that implies that you could sell out. But of course, it just reflected their reality, that they've seen people sell out or abandon them."

Carlos Beristain described the meeting that about 60 relatives of the disappeared students attended. They received the experts with a live band and freshly made flower wreaths: a traditional Guerrero welcoming of honor. Beristain said that one by one the different family members took the microphone and addressed the five experts.

"They all said three things," Beristain told me: "Always tell us the truth, you have our trust, and—and this really hit me—please, don't sell out."

I spoke with Isabel Alcaraz Alcaraz, mother of Bernardo Flores Alcaraz, a few days after that meeting and asked her for her initial impressions of the expert group.

"I think it went well," she said of the meeting. "They explained to us how they planned to work and I personally, as well as what I've heard the others saying, thought that, okay, we have another hope because we saw how they explained to us their way of working, their plans, and we all thought that it would lead to good results. They told us they were completely independent and that they would be working collectively, independently of the government."

By July 2015, when I first began to assemble the oral history that would become this book, it was still more common to encounter confusion, rumors, speculation, and disinformation about the attacks in the media than direct descriptions of the events from those who had lived through them. The government, much of the media, and even many activists in solidarity with the students still spoke of the students having been riding on four buses, though they were aboard five buses when attacked. They also spoke of only one scene of attack from which police disappeared students, but this was done during simultaneous attacks, from two distinct locations: the corner of Juan N. Álvarez and Periférico Norte and in front of the Guerrero state courthouse, called the Palacio de Justicia. People still spoke of the students having been attacked for having protested the DIF event in Iguala, even though it had been long since proven that no such protest took place.

The GIEI released its first report in September 2015. The report confirmed not only the participation of state and federal police in the attacks, but also that of municipal police from the neighboring municipalities of Cocula and Huitzuco. It also included testimony of a military intelligence agent (a document that the independent investigators found amongst the 85 volumes and more than 80,000 pages of the federal government's case file at that moment) who was present at one of the scenes where police attacked and disappeared the 43 students, observing and reporting in real time to his superiors. The GIEI report also documented both the torture of almost everyone arrested by federal authorities in the case and the particular institutional mechanisms for sanctioning that torture.

Among the other key findings, the GIEI discovered official video camera evidence of one of the scenes of attack where police disappeared some 15 to 20 students in front of the state courthouse on the highway leading out of town. That video, however, was—supposedly—retrieved and then destroyed because a state judge said she didn't see anything of value in the video. For this judge, a video of police attacking unarmed students who were all disappeared was nothing of value. Or, what really happened to that video? Was it destroyed, or hidden? Either way, how could that happen? Or, more to the point, what does the government's self-proclaimed destruction of evidence documenting police attacking and disappearing college students reveal to us about the nature and function of that government?

The GIEI also emphasized that the students had been attacked aboard five buses, and that the fifth bus, the Estrella Roja bus, was *itself* also disappeared. When the experts asked the government to see that bus, the government officials showed them a different bus and lied repeatedly. The experts proved that the Estrella Roja bus the students rode that night and the bus provided by the government were different, using video images from the bus station's security cameras (which federal detectives had not even bothered to look at).

Upon realizing that the "fifth bus" was missing and that the government had tried to lie and manipulate its way around providing that bus, the experts asked some more questions: Could there have been something on that particular bus so valuable that it provoked the attacks? Could there have been, for example, a major heroin shipment hidden in secret compartments on the bus? Is that why the government can't show anyone the real bus? Guerrero state is one of the largest heroin-producing regions in the world. Iguala is a known trafficking hub for heroin bound for the United States. Could the Ayotzinapa students have unwittingly grabbed a bus loaded with heroin bound for, say, Chicago? Could that have provoked the heroin shippers to order the recovery of the bus and the murders and disappearances of the students? If so, what does that say about the relationship between police—not one or two "corrupt" cops, but all on-duty municipal, state, and federal police officers in Iguala, acting together under the watchful eye of military intelligence agents only two miles down the road from a major army base—and the transnational heroin trade?

Rather than address such questions, the media focused on the GIEI's thorough debunking of the federal attorney general's claim that three confessed "drug gang" members murdered and incinerated the 43 students at an open-air trash dump in Cocula between 3:00 a.m. and 5:00 p.m. on September 27, 2014. The GIEI concluded, based on an in-depth forensic fire analysis, that no such fire occurred, and, moreover, that such a fire would have incinerated not only the 43 students, but all of the surrounding vegetation in the dump, likely causing a forest fire as well as killing any human who approached the flames to feed them more wood and tires, as the supposed killers claimed (under torture) they did.

The GIEI's findings unleashed a kind of media war of fire experts. Several newspaper columnists began a slander campaign against the GIEI, claiming that they were only in Mexico for the money, and that two members had connections to armed guerrilla groups in Guatemala and Colombia. The GIEI later released satellite images of the trash dump from September 26 and 27, 2014. The images are clear: it was raining, there was no raging cremation pyre used to reduce 43 human bodies to ash. In November 2014 and again in June 2015, I spoke with two Cocula municipal trash workers. They both said that they dumped the trash in Cocula on September 27, 2014, around 1:00 p.m. The ground was still wet from the rain, they told me, and there was no one there. There was no fire. In early 2016, the Argentine forensic anthropologists would confirm all these findings in their own independent report based on more than a year's inch-by-inch analysis of the Cocula trash dump: there was no major fire incinerating even one person, much less 43 people, there on the night of September 26–27, 2014, or any other day between then and the end of October when the analysts began their work.

After the publication of the GIEI's first report, the federal government, which had already extended the group's mandate by another six months, grew cold toward the five experts. Soon thereafter more and more slanderous reports began to appear in the government-friendly press attacking the experts, claiming that they were sympathetic with "subversive" groups and were "anti-military." From the very beginning of its investigation, the GIEI formally requested to interview the soldiers of the 27th Batallion present in Iguala on September 26–27, 2014. The government flatly refused to let the GIEI experts carry out those interviews. National Defense Secretary Salvador Cienfuegos told a Televisa reporter on October 6, 2015, "I cannot allow the soldiers to be treated like criminals" and implied that the members of the GIEI "want to interrogate the soldiers so as to later make it seem like they were involved" in the attacks.

The army's role in the attacks presents a striking enigma. With a large military base (which was involved in the forced disappearances and counterinsurgency campaigns of the 1960s and 1970s) located one mile away from the scene, why didn't soldiers intervene on behalf of the students who were under attack for hours? As confirmed in the GIEI reports, the army—formally tasked with combating organized crime across the country—had been monitoring the movements of the students using highway surveillance equipment since 6:00 p.m. on September 26.

A military intelligence agent also reported to his superiors from one of the main scenes of the mass forced disappearances in real time. Army officers knew exactly what was happening. When soldiers finally were deployed sometime around 1:00 a.m., they proceeded to lecture the students hiding in a private clinic about the value of making good grades while Edgar Vargas nearly bled to death from a bullet wound to the face. How to explain the army's apparent refusal to respond to or investigate the disappearances, the shootings, and the murders that continued to take place throughout the night? Was the army's non-response to the police attacks that night a decision rather than a failure? If so, who made that decision, who gave the orders that night, and why? Did the federal government refuse to let the GIEI speak with soldiers because they have something to hide? If so, what are they hiding?

The students of Ayotzinapa, who were so demonized by government officials and the commercial press, were among the very few people who acted as if there existed something called "the rule of law" that night. After the police attacked the students on Juan N. Álvarez Street, after they abducted and drove off with some 20 students there, a commanding officer threatened the remaining students if they didn't leave the city, saying: *We'll come back for you.* The students, however, defied the threat and remained in the area to support the students whom they thought had been arrested. They planned to protest the following day to demand that the arrested be released. As one student, Carlos Martínez, said, they *couldn't even imagine* that the police would kill them, much less that the police would disappear 43 of their *compañeros.* They assumed that the police would act according to the law, even though they had already violated the law during the attacks.

The students viewed the space around them as a "crime scene" and sought to protect the integrity of "evidence" such as spent bullet casings, bullet holes in the buses, and pools of blood on the street and in the third bus. The students phoned the press; they also called their schoolmates in Ayotzinapa. Between around 10:30 p.m. and midnight, the students waited for the "authorities" to arrive. During that time, several groups of people arrived at the scene, including two vans full of students from the school, teachers from the CETEG, and six Iguala reporters. No government officials arrived. No one from the army base located one mile away arrived. No one from the state or federal police investigative units arrived. Local police maintained wide checkpoints at all the roads leading in and out of town, but none came to Juan N. Álvarez or the state courthouse to investigate what had happened there. Not a single government official arrived to carry out their supposed legal duties. It was the students of Ayotzinapa who behaved—to their mortal danger—as if a "rule of law" existed, by safeguarding "evidence" and waiting for the proper "authorities" to arrive. Three men in face masks armed with assault rifles did show up and open fire on the students giving a press conference. Those men killed two students—Julio César Ramírez Nava and Daniel Solís—and shot Edgar Vargas in the mouth. Julio César Mondragón Fontes was last seen alive running from those masked attackers.

The GIEI published its second and final report in April 2016. The families of the disappeared students clamored for its investigation to continue. The Mexican federal government, however, refused to sign another six-month extension of the agreement, effectively kicking the five experts out of the country.[11] The experts knew this as they prepared their second and final report. The report further detailed a series of government actions in the investigation that appeared to hover in a difficult-to-discern area between extreme ineptitude and sinister malfeasance. But the bombshell, so to speak, was a series of photographs and video images showing the supposed lead federal investigator Tomás Zerón de Lucio at the San Juan River, near the Cocula trash dump, on October 28, 2014. I say "supposed" because one federal attorney told me that Zerón's job itself was illegal, that he did not even have a permit to carry a handgun, and he did not have the legal authority to conduct crime scene investigations, much less with one of the accused at an investigation site without his attorney.

In the photographs and video we see Zerón, armed, pointing and leading a number of detectives while another armed man in a suit leads the accused around the river. At one moment we see a black trash bag by the river. Zerón indicates that the other officers should check it out, see if it has human remains in it. A man is then seen sticking his hand into the bag and pulling out clumps of some substance (human ash?) and sifting that substance in the river. So much for proper handling of evidence.

One thing that was so striking about the images, however, was the date: October 28, 2014. This was important because the federal government said that agents found the bag of ash on October 29, 2014. Simple confusion? Probably

---

11. It would later be revealed that spyware sold to the Mexican government was used around this time to hack the cellphones of and spy on members of the GIEI as well as lawyers from the Miguel Austín Pro Juárez Human Rights Center representing the parents of the disappeared, murdered, and wounded students. See Azam Ahmed, "Spyware Sold to the Mexican Government Targeted International Officials," *New York Times*, July 10, 2017, p. A1.

not, since the search that was conducted on October 29, 2014, was rigorously documented and entered into the case file. There was absolutely nothing, however, in the case file from the activities carried out on October 28, 2014. It would seem then, that two freelance reporters, Daniel Villa and José Manuel Jiménez—who chose to follow the police to the trash dump that day and photograph and film from a distance using telephoto lenses, and who couldn't even get their work from that day published—filmed the supposed lead federal detective carrying out a dress rehearsal for the following day's "discovery." That is, the federal government planting evidence and rehearsing testimonies.

The two GIEI reports, together totaling 1,030 pages, make up perhaps the single most rigorously documented description of how impunity itself is carefully elaborated by the Mexican federal government. Impunity is not the result of "corruption" or "incompetence" or a "lack of resources." Impunity is an exquisitely crafted function of the judicial system; it is in fact the defining feature of the judicial system. Or, as I once heard writer Francisco Goldman say at a journalism conference in Guadalajara: "Impunity is the freedom of expression of the killers."

In addition to the two GIEI reports, one of the five experts, Carlos Beristain, published a book in 2017 called *El tiempo de Ayotzinapa*, or *Ayotzinapa Time*, about his experiences investigating the attacks against the students. In the book Beristain tells from personal experience the tales of impunity documented in the two GIEI reports. Among many other details, he writes about the testimony of one of the bus drivers describing the participation of Guerrero state and Huitzuco municipal police in the attacks; the destruction of the courthouse video that recorded one of the two scenes of mass forced disappearance at the hands of the police; the immediately apparent contradictions in the government's trash dump hypothesis; the absurdity of the government's claim to have found 41 bullet casings piled up on top of a rock in the trash dump after detectives, independent forensic experts, and journalists had spent a week combing the dump for evidence; how Jorge Aníbal Cruz Mendoza sent his mother a text message at 1:16 a.m. on September 27 asking her to add credit to his phone, when, according to the federal government, all the students had been murdered by that time; how, nine months after the attacks, one of the experts, Claudia Paz y Paz, found a note in the case file describing the clothing of the students disappeared from the bus in front of the courthouse and how detectives had thrown all the clothing clumped together in plastic bags without conducting any forensic analyses and without even telling the families or their lawyers that they had found such clothing; how Ángela Buitrago working in the predawn hours found a handwritten signed testimony of the driver of the Estrella Roja "fifth bus" stating—as the students had—that the bus was stopped by federal police, that police ordered the students off the bus, that the police escorted the bus to the outskirts of Iguala and told the driver to call his boss and then go to Jojutla and then Cuautla, in Morelos state, where the driver arrived at 5:00 a.m., wrote his testimony by hand, and signed it, which contradicts the federal government's multiple and mutually contradictory statements about that bus and what happened to it; and how then–federal attorney general Arely Gómez lied to the world when she falsely claimed in a press conference that the remains of a second student, Jhosivani de la Cruz, had been positively identified at the lab in Austria: no such identification had been made.[12]

---

12. Carlos Beristain. 2017. *El tiempo de Ayotzinapa*, Madrid: Akal. pp. 68–69, 82–83, 97–98, 105–106, 129–130, 137–139.

The GIEI's revelations led to a short-lived scandal concerning the actions of Tomás Zerón de Lucio on October 28, 2014. Two weeks before the second anniversary of the attacks against the students, President Enrique Peña Nieto left no doubt as to the role of the highest levels of the federal government in the forced disappearances of the 43 students. On September 14, 2016, Tomás Zerón resigned from the agency inside the federal attorney general's office in charge of the Ayotzinapa investigation. And then, hours later, the president promoted him: on September 14, 2016, Peña Nieto appointed Zerón to be the Technical Secretary of the National Security Council, a job that answers directly to the president. The man who had been overseeing the torture of detainees, the fabrication of evidence, and a myriad of lies and deceptions would now be in charge of the President's National Security Council. The message was quite clear.

The government's false narrative attempts to depoliticize the attacks by denying the violence directly perpetrated by the Mexican army, federal police, and state police. Instead, the government narrative attempts to localize the atrocities, focusing exclusively on the Iguala and Cocula police, alleged "cartel members," and former Iguala mayor José Luis Abarca and his wife, María de los Ángeles Pineda. This narrative serves to perpetuate the essential drug war myth that a genuine separation exists between so-called drug cartels and the government. The neatly packaged government story describing how "corrupt" local police working for a narco power couple grabbed the students and "turned them over" to bad-guy narcos makes it seem—contrary to all available evidence—that the "narcos" are to blame, and a stronger federal police and military presence is needed to protect people from them. An overwhelming amount of evidence describes a very different reality: on September 26–27, 2014, scores of Iguala, Cocula, and Huitzuco police collaborated with Guerrero state police and federal police to carry out hours of horrific violence against unarmed college students while the Mexican army watched from the shadows.

For, even though the government arrested more than 120 Iguala and Cocula police officers, local officials, Abarca and Pineda, as well as supposed "gang" members, all of those arrests support its official version of both the attacks and the fate of the students. Santiago Aguirre, the Miguel Agustín Pro Juárez human rights attorney representing the families, told me that all of the people arrested have been charged with bogus crimes. More than half have been charged with generic crimes unrelated to the attacks against the students, like "organized crime" or "drug trafficking."Those arrested in direct connection to the attacks have been charged not with murder and forced disappearance, but with "kidnapping." Moreover, all of the government's charges relate to the attacks on Juan N. Álvarez street. The government has not charged a single person in connection to the mass forced disappearance of students in front of the state courthouse: the location from which the government video footage was destroyed (or hidden) and at which the military intelligence agent was present.

And yet, after the GIEI's two reports, a number of things have been forcefully established about the federal government's version of events. Chief among them: 1) neither the students nor anyone else was incinerated in the Cocula trash dump on September 26–27, 2014; and 2) the Mexican federal attorney general's office, under the tenures of Jesús Murillo Karam and Arely Gómez and the guidance of Tomás Zerón, invented a fake crime scene, tortured the accused into signing and repeating false confessions related to that scene, hid the Estrella Roja bus and then lied about it, and planted evidence—including a bone fragment that was identified as belonging to the student Alexander Mora Venancio—at the banks of the knee-deep San Juan River.

Many unanswered questions remain, including: how did federal investigators, including Tomás Zerón, get their hands on what has been identified as a charred bone fragment from Alexander Mora Venancio's body?

After the ceremony in Mexico City where the GIEI publicly presented its second report, the five experts went back to Ayotzinapa for their final meeting with the families.

"I mean, fuck. We had finished our term. The government threw us out. The families would still be there, on their own. And we didn't tell them where their sons were," Francisco Cox told me in Mexico City after the meeting. "And so I stood up, and I told them that if, I mean, it was. . . . We had given the best of ourselves, and truly our reports contain solid lines for further investigation; they're well documented, and could be the guide that the families should use in moving forward. But I couldn't deny that I felt . . . a pain that . . . for not being able to tell them . . . where their sons are. . . . And, um . . . That's when everyone started crying."

The term "cover-up" is too generous. To this day, the Mexican federal government continues to disappear the 43 students, among many thousands of other Mexicans and Central American migrants who have been forcibly disappeared, often by the very people authorized and paid to "serve and protect" them.

Forced disappearances have two stages. The material stage occurs when police, soldiers, or armed actors physically abduct someone, as the police did with the 43 students, and take them away to an undisclosed destination. The legal-administrative stage occurs when government officials create a false narrative, and then perpetrate new atrocities to support it. In the case of the attacks against the Azotzinapa students, officials tortured people to create false confessions, fabricated a false crime scene, destroyed essential forensic evidence, planted false evidence, and propagated false accounts by feeding disinformation to the press. During the legal-administrative stage of forced disappearance the perpetrators attempt to disappear the truth—any and all verifyable knowledge about the events—along with the bodies of those being disappeared. While the police use guns, patrol vehicles, roads, radios, mobile phones, and other tools to disappear people, the legal administrators of forced disappearance employ computers, the mass media, government office space, public funds, laboratories, maps, graphs, texts and all manner of legal documents to do the same. The government officials in suits who created reams of documents to sustain lies are just as responsible for the forced disappearances as the uniformed police who physically abducted the 43 students.

And that is not all. Those officials, including the lawyers, detectives, and politicians, have been torturing—literally, torturing—the families of the disappeared daily from September 27, 2014, to the present day. Every time these officials lie and go before the television cameras with their detailed descriptions of the students being thrown into a fire, their descriptions of the killers feeding the flames with gasoline and old tires, every time they tell that lie they force the mothers and fathers to imagine their children meeting such an end, when we—and they—know that said fire never burned. As Mario César González Contreras, father of César Manuel González Hernández, said at a press conference after the GIEI presented their first report on September 6, 2015: "From day one the trash dump has been torture for the families of the 43 disappeared students!"

María de Jesús Tlatempa Bello, mother of José Eduardo Bartolo Tlatempa, said that same day:

"Today it was shown that we were right and that we are the victims of our own government. Today it was proven that the government lies. And the first one to do so was Ángel Aguirre when he told us that our children were in the mass graves in Pueblo Viejo. Imagine what immense pain for a mother to be told such falsehood, such a vile lie! Today we know that he lied. And then the federal attorney general told us that our sons ended up in the trash dump, that those 43 young men had been incinerated. But we never believed him."

And during that same press conference, Bernabé Abraján, father of Adán Abraján de la Cruz, said that he and other parents had gone to the Cocula trash dump two days after the government had first inspected the area. "And we realized that there was nothing there. We now know that the government has been lying to us," he said. "We, the mothers and fathers of the 43 students from Ayotzinapa, we are all *campesinos*. And the truth is that this government wanted to step all over our dignity, and that of our sons. Since the day of the twenty-sixth, we have been struggling to find our children. This government thought that we would give up, because at the beginning it tried to buy us off. It offered us money. But we, as *campesinos* and the parents of our children, told the government that we wouldn't sell our children. Our children are our children and they are not for sale. That's why we are fighting to find the 43 students. And this government needs to realize that we will not give up. . . . We don't know anything about legal matters. But we know what dignity is."

Names of the Murdered, Coma Victim, and Disappeared in Iguala, Guerrero, on September 26–27, 2014

Killed in Iguala
1. Julio César Mondragón Fontes, 22, Ayotzinapa student
2. Daniel Solís Gallardo, 18, Ayotzinapa student
3. Julio César Ramírez Nava, 23, Ayotzinapa student
4. David Josué García Evangelista, 15, soccer player
5. Víctor Manuel Lugo Ortiz, 50, soccer team bus driver
6. Blanca Montiel Sánchez, 40, taxi passenger on the highway

In a coma with a shot to the head
Aldo Gutiérrez Solano, 19, Ayotzinapa student

Ayotzinapa students forcibly disappeared
1. Abel García Hernández, 19
2. Abelardo Vázquez Penitén, 19
3. Adán Abraján de la Cruz, 20
4. Alexander Mora Venancio, 19
5. Antonio Santana Maestro, 19
6. Benjamín Ascencio Bautista, 19
7. Bernardo Flores Alcaraz, 21
8. Carlos Iván Ramírez Villarreal, 20
9. Carlos Lorenzo Hernández Muñoz, 19
10. César Manuel González Hernández, 19
11. Christian Alfonso Rodríguez Telumbre, 21
12. Christian Tomás Colón Garnica, 18

13. Cutberto Ortiz Ramos, 22
14. Doriam González Parral, 19
15. Emiliano Alen Gaspar de la Cruz, 23
16. Everardo Rodríguez Bello, 21
17. Felipe Arnulfo Rosas, 20
18. Giovanni Galindes Guerrero, 20
19. Israel Caballero Sánchez, 19
20. Israel Jacinto Lugardo, 19
21. Jesús Jovany Rodríguez Tlatempa, 21
22. Jonás Trujillo González, 20
23. Jorge Álvarez Nava, 19
24. Jorge Aníbal Cruz Mendoza, 19
25. Jorge Antonio Tizapa Legideño, 20
26. Jorge Luis González Parral, 21
27. José Ángel Campos Cantor, 33
28. José Ángel Navarrete González, 18
29. José Eduardo Bartolo Tlatempa, 17
30. José Luis Luna Torres, 20
31. Jhosivani Guerrero de la Cruz, 20
32. Julio César López Patolzin, 25
33. Leonel Castro Abarca, 18
34. Luis Ángel Abarca Carrillo, 20
35. Luis Ángel Francisco Arzola, 20
36. Magdaleno Rubén Lauro Villegas, 19
37. Marcial Pablo Baranda, 20
38. Marco Antonio Gómez Molina, 20
39. Martín Getsemany Sánchez García, 20
40. Mauricio Ortega Valerio, 18
41. Miguel Ángel Hernández Martínez, 27
42. Miguel Ángel Mendoza Zacarías, 23
43. Saúl Bruno García, 20

ACKNOWLEDGMENTS

Thanks with all my heart to everyone who spoke with me and shared their stories for this book and to all the families and the Ayotzinapa students who have continued their tireless search and struggle for the disappeared, the fallen, the wounded, the truth, and justice; and to all those in solidarity who helped me during the months of reporting in Guerrero: Kau Sirenio, Marcela Turati, Sergio Ocampo, Lenin Ocampo, Ulises Domínguez, Vania Pigeonutt, Margena de la O, Jesús Guerrero, María Benítez, Daniela Rea, Norma González, Edith Victorino, Naira, Füsun, Almazán, Diego, Sandra, Meño y Nayeli, Ray y Yuri, Adriana, Alba, A., Andrés y Sara, Enrique, Andalucía, Francesca, Eileen, Elia y Luz, Diana y Matt, Sánchez, Valencia y Tania, Paco y Jovi, Nel, Lolita, Emiliano, Río Doce, Ana Paula, M., C., Raúl, Thalía, Témoris, Valin, David Espino, Alejandro Guerrero, Natividad Ambrocio, Muki, Maya Telumbre, Pablo Rojas, Patricia Salinas, Daniel Alarcón, Ted Lewis, Kit Rachlis, Douglas McGray, *California Sunday Magazine*, Suzanne Gollin, Valentina López DeCea, Edith López Ovalle, Fernanda Gómez, Paula Mónaco y todas las compañeras y los compañeros de H.I.J.O.S. México, and Greg, Elaine, Bob, Stacey, Chris, Linda, Elizabeth, and everyone at City Lights Books.

ABOUT THE AUTHOR

JOHN GIBLER lives and writes in Mexico. He is the author of *Mexico Unconquered: Chronicles of Power and Revolt*, *To Die in Mexico: Dispatches From Inside the Drug War*, *20 poemas para ser leídos en una balacera*, and *Tzompaxtle: La fuga de un guerrillero*, forthcoming in English as *Torn from the World: A Guerrilla's Escape from a Secret Prison in Mexico*.

ARIEL DORFMAN is a Chilean-American author whose plays (among them, *Death and the Maiden*), have been performed in more than 100 countries and whose numerous books (novels, stories, poems, essays) have been translated into more than 60 languages. Accompanied by his wife, Angélica, Ariel divides his time between Chile and the United States, where he is professor emeritus of literature at Duke University. He is a regular contributor to the most important newspapers worldwide. His latest novel is *Darwin's Ghosts*.

NEW AND FORTHCOMING IN THE OPEN MEDIA SERIES

Torn from the World
A Guerrilla's Escape from a Secret Prison in Mexico
By John Gibler

Have Black Lives Ever Mattered?
By Mumia Abu-Jamal

Storming the Wall
Climate Change, Migration, and Homeland Security
By Todd Miller

Loaded
A Disarming History of the Second Amendment
By Roxanne Dunbar-Ortiz

American Nightmare
The Challenge of U.S. Authoritarianism
By Henry A. Giroux

Violence
Humans in Dark Times
By Brad Evans and Natasha Lennard

Because We Say So
Noam Chomsky

The Fire and the Word
A History of the Zapatista Movement
By Gloria Muñoz Ramírez

Dying to Live
A Story of U.S. Immigration in an Age of Global Apartheid
Joseph Nevins

CITY LIGHTS BOOKS | OPEN MEDIA SERIES
ARM YOURSELF WITH INFORMATION